Real Life Bully Prevention for Real Kids

50 Ways to Help Elementary and Middle School Students

CATHERINE DePINO

ROWMAN & LITTLEFIELD EDUCATION
Lanham • New York • Toronto • Plymouth, UK

Published in the United States of America
by Rowman & Littlefield Education
A Division of Rowman & Littlefield Publishers, Inc.
A wholly owned subsidary of The Rowman & Littlefield Publishing Group, Inc.
4501 Forbes Boulevard, Suite 200, Lanham, Maryland 20706
www.rowmaneducation.com

Estover Road
Plymouth PL6 7PY
United Kingdom

Copyright © 2009 by Catherine DePino

British Library Cataloguing in Publication Information Available

Library of Congress Cataloging-in-Publication Data

DePino, Catherine.
  Real life bully prevention for real kids : 50 ways to help elementary and middle school students / Catherine DePino.
      p. cm.
  ISBN-13: 978-1-57886-965-7 (cloth : alk. paper)
  ISBN-10: 1-57886-965-X (cloth : alk. paper)
  ISBN-13: 978-1-57886-967-1(electronic)
  ISBN-10: 1-57886-967-6 (electronic)
  1. Bullying in schools—Prevention. 2. School children—Crimes against—
Prevention. I. Title.
  LB3013.3.D455 2009
  372.15'8—dc22   2008035203

⊗™ The paper used in this publication meets the minimum requirements of American National Standard for Information Sciences—Permanence of Paper for Printed Library Materials, ANSI/NISO Z39.48-1992.
Manufactured in the United States of America.

To my mother, Mary Grace Spinelli,
my first and best teacher

Mom, thank you for teaching me
about the colors and textures of
words, the warmth of a lasting
friendship, and the comfort of
unconditional love.

—Catherine Spinelli DePino

Contents

LEVEL 3 ACTIVITIES: ADVANCED

Acknowledgments

My deepest appreciation to Dr. Thomas Koerner, a gentleman and a scholar, for his kindness and understanding in supporting this project from start to finish. I'm also grateful to Maera Winters, editorial assistant, for her expert guidance. Thanks to my highly creative production editor, Krista Sprecher, for helping me bring this book to publication, and to Paul Cacciato, assistant editor, for always being helpful.

Foreword

As the director of psychology training at the NYU Child Study Center and in my clinical practice, I see a myriad of children whose lives are affected by bullying. While bullying is clearly not a new problem, we now have evidence that seeing it as "part of growing up" is a mistake. The negative long-lasting effects of being a victim, bystander, or bully are well documented. Bullying continues to be a major issue in our schools with the fear and anxiety created by an environment in which bullying occurs, negatively impacting learning and social development. A significant number of students miss school on a regular basis out of fear of being bullied.

The groundbreaking research conducted by Dan Olweus (1993), involving over 150,000 students in grades one through nine in Scandinavia and now replicated in sites across the United States, has documented that interventions taking place in a therapy office or with individuals are clearly not sufficient.

For bully reduction to be effective, SCHOOL is the venue. Effective programs must recognize bullying as a problem; involve students, staff, and parents; and generally create a culture in which bullying is unacceptable. In my work with schools, it is clear that for schools to adopt such programs the designers need to have an in-depth understanding not only of effective bully reduction techniques but also an understanding of the school environment, sound educational practices, and activities in line with other educational objectives of the school. Catherine DePino's book ably shows how to accomplish that complex task.

I had the pleasure of meeting Catherine DePino when she was a guest on our satellite radio show, *About Our Kids*, on Sirius "Doctor Radio." I invited her to speak about her published and forthcoming children's books on the topic of bullying. The fiction books, especially *Blue Cheese Breath and Stinky Feet*, my personal favorite, help children begin a dialogue on bullying with characters they can relate to and places them in the realm of experiences that are sadly all too familiar.

I have used *Blue Cheese Breath and Stinky Feet* many times in clinical practice as well as recommended it to parents and school personnel. When I found out that she was writing *Real Life Bully Prevention for Real Kids*, I was genuinely excited as this type of publication would serve as an invaluable resource to teachers and school administrators who recognize the need to address the issue of bullying in their schools.

Dr. DePino's book offers user-friendly help to schools and educators who recognize the importance of their role in reducing the negative effects on individuals and communities of being a bully victim or a bystander. In her book, she offers well thought-out activities aligned with the current research on effective bully reduction programs. But what makes this book especially valuable is her intimate understanding of classrooms and school structure.

Her activities are written in lesson plan format, making them easy to integrate into any classroom. Her understanding of cognitive development makes the activities age and grade level appropriate. Furthermore, the variety of groupings is in line with the pedagogy of cooperative learning, a particularly useful context to implement curriculum centered on the development of appropriate social skills. Dr. DePino's sensitivity to different types of learning styles is clearly evident and makes the activities engaging, at times challenging, and always informative.

Furthermore, in the ever-evolving world in which our children come of age, *Real Life Bully Prevention for Real Kids* manages to remain timely. Unfortunately, one of the negative side effects to the cyber era is the phenomenon of cyber bullying. Catherine DePino's book addresses this issue as well as taking into account the new and different challenges it presents and the need for schools to take it on as well. This farsighted approach to a problem long misunderstood is indicative of the clarity and insight the author brings to her subject.

I have no doubt that *Real Life Bully Prevention for Real Kids* will be an amazing resource for teachers and schools in general. Ultimately, I hope Dr. DePino's book will be the beginning of a path to schools being more kind and accepting places for kids to learn and grow. I look forward to seeing the next publication of the products produced with some of the activities in the book. Maybe a bully reduction rap in the top 40?

Dr. Lori Evans

Dr. Lori Evans is director of training at the NYU Medical Center Psychology program. A specialist in ADHD and behavior disorders, Dr. Evans has coordinated the "Treatment of Adolescent Suicide Attempters" study at the NYU Child Study Center and has appeared on several TV programs, including ABC and NBC News.

How to Use This Book:
Note to Teachers

Real Life Bully Prevention for Real Kids: 50 Ways to Help Elementary and Middle School Students gives teachers—particularly those teaching English, social studies, or health education—practical bully-prevention activities for the entire class, small groups, and individuals. You can fit each of these related activities into one or more class periods, lengthening or shortening them according to your individual time constraints.

Real Life Bully Prevention for Real Kids offers hands-on bully-prevention activities. Each activity contains a description, goals for students in the "Teaches" section, and helpful hints for teachers. The book's user-friendly format helps teachers attain curricular goals for bully prevention and character education, with the added bonus of improving reading, writing, and speaking skills.

All activities include related segments for the entire class, small groups (or partners), and individuals. You may want to assign some of the individual activities for homework, encouraging parents, siblings, and grandparents to participate actively in your school's bully prevention program. Each segment reinforces the student objectives and gives extra practice in bully prevention.

The activities are both teacher and student friendly in that they are easy for teachers to facilitate and for students to carry out. Before students begin each activity, you may want to use the many examples throughout the book as models to motivate students to generate their own ideas. You may also want to read the examples to spark further discussion and debate about each of the topics. The activities, which are grouped in three levels of complexity, challenge students of different age and ability levels and may be expanded or modified to fit your student population.

You can easily adapt the activities to fit a variety of grades, abilities, and learning styles. You can also tailor the activities to your individual classroom settings: for example, you may want to set up the small group instruction for partners if that works better for you.

In short, *Real Life Bully Prevention for Real Kids* offers enlightening, enjoyable activities that give students many ways to deal with different types of bullies.

> The world is a dangerous place, not because of those who do evil, but because of those who look on and do nothing.
>
> Albert Einstein

LEVEL I ACTIVITIES: BASIC

ACTIVITY 1

Brainstorm Anti-bullying Tips

Description: Brainstorm your best ideas to counteract common bullying problems. Groups discuss their ideas with the class. Write a journal entry about bullying problems and solutions.

Teaches: Character education (self-reliance in dealing with problems); problem solving; writing (journaling) to generate solutions to problems; speaking in front of groups; and logical progression of ideas.

Helpful Hints: Before you begin the activity, discuss types of bullying situations the children have experienced or witnessed in school, on the playground, cafeteria, on the bus, or in their neighborhoods.

School and playground bullying may include a child ridiculing a classmate who gets good grades; a classmate in an inclusion class blocking a special needs child from going down a sliding board; or a group of students excluding a child from a game.

Bullying in the cafeteria includes throwing food at another student or telling another child he or she cannot sit at a certain table.

Neighborhood bullying may include ignoring other children or not inviting them to participate in group activities.

Ask what types of responses to the episodes have worked best to diffuse the situations and to prevent them from happening in the future.

Entire Class

1. Have the class brainstorm a bullying situation they've experienced or have seen others experience. Write (or have a student write) each situation on the board. Leave enough space to write possible solutions to each bullying problem. Here are two examples: a classmate demands to look at your test answers or someone calls you a name or hits you.

2. Ask the class to brainstorm a list of things they would be willing to try in order to cope with each bullying episode. As the class dictates, write the corresponding ideas on the board next to each situation.

Sample List

Situation	Possible Solution
A classmate demands to look at your history test answers.	Ignore the person or shake your head *no*.
A boy calls you a terrible name.	Say, "I don't like that" and walk away.
A girl punches you for no reason.	Tell an adult you trust.

Have the class vote on the three best solutions to each problem. Ask students to explain why they believe these solutions would work best.

Small Groups

1. Students meet in small groups to brainstorm bullying problems they've experienced or witnessed at school, at home, or in the neighborhood.

Examples

school: teasing someone because of appearance

home: bullying a sibling or another relative

neighborhood: ignoring or making fun of other children

Groups discuss possible solutions to each problem.

2. Each group chooses its two best situations and solutions and explains them to the class. Allow ten to fifteen minutes for each group to report their ideas for solving the problem listed. Leave time for discussion.

Individuals

Class members will relate a bullying situation they or a friend have experienced, or one they've heard about, and will write a journal entry describing the problem's solution. Volunteers will tell the entire class their ideas for dealing with the problem they've listed. Class members will then give their own ideas for solutions to the problem.

Sample Journal Entry

Last week a group of girls at the next table told another girl who was overweight that they didn't want her sitting with them. They told her that she had greasy hair and smelled bad and that they didn't want her around. The girl looked like she was going to cry and got up to leave. A friend at my table said, "You can sit with us."

When she got to our table, my friend said, "You don't want to be around those girls if they treat you that way." My friend taught me that it's important for people who see someone being bullied to get involved and to help in any way they can. Who knows when a bully will bother them and they'll need help?

ACTIVITY 2

Write a Magazine Article about Stopping Bullying Before It Starts

Description: List specific things you can do to prevent others from bullying you before it starts. Refer to the list when your group writes short magazine articles. Write a letter of encouragement to a person facing bullying.

Teaches: Proactive bully prevention; character education (empathy for those facing bullying and becoming part of the solution for bullying problems); writing magazine articles about bully prevention; and deciding how to best disseminate bully prevention ideas to others.

Helpful Hints:

Explain what it means to be proactive, to stop something before it has a chance to start. With bullies, it often means avoiding or ignoring them.

Discuss examples in which students have been successful in preventing bullying or have seen others stop it by thinking ahead. Ask the class to list feeling words they might experience if they prevented a bully from striking.

Examples

happy
satisfied
excited
relieved

Ask the class to think about situations in which it was impossible to avoid a bully. Suppose they did everything to avoid a bully and the person still harassed them. How should they react? What would they do next?

Entire Class

1. Discuss the importance of being prepared *before* a bully strikes. Ask the class to think creatively about how they can prevent bullies from bothering them. Start them off with some ideas: for example, avoid places where you know bullies might show up; build a strong support system of friends; don't be alone when the bully's around; stay near friends if you think someone's around who might bother you; keep a low profile with someone who has bullied you in the past; stand and walk with strength and confidence; keep your voice steady and calm, and walk away from the bully if you can. If none of these things work and the bullying persists or gets worse, ask an adult you trust for help.

2. Write all the ideas on the board, and have the students debate why each one would work or not work. Ask them to explain why some suggestions would work in certain circumstances and not in others.

3. Discuss why writing a short magazine article might be a positive way to help stop bullying before it starts.

Sample Answers

It's brief and makes its point quickly.
It's easy to understand and use.
Other students can easily learn from it.

Small Groups

1. Small groups will write short, age-appropriate children's magazine articles. They will illustrate the articles with their own drawings or pictures cut from magazines. They will write an original title:

Examples

Clip a Bully's Wings
Who's Afraid of a Big, Bad Bully?
Stop Bullying Before it Starts
Break the Bullying Chain.

2. Groups will design and illustrate a magazine cover for the article, giving their magazine a title and featuring their article with a one-sentence blurb on the cover.

3. Students will incorporate at least five suggestions for preventing bullying in the article (two ideas they learned from the class discussion and three original ideas) and explain how they'll implement these suggestions.

4. They will end their articles with words of encouragement to students who want to learn how to stop bullying before it begins.

5. Ask students how they think they can make the most effective use of their articles.

Examples

Distribute them to other classes.
Ask the local newspaper to print segments of articles, possibly with a feature article about bullying.
Sponsor a newspaper or schoolwide contest to choose the best article.

6. Work with another teacher to have your classes compose articles that stress proactive bully prevention techniques. Display articles outside your classrooms and on parents' night.

Individuals

Using one idea from the group's articles, students will write a letter of encouragement to a real or imaginary student who has started experiencing mistreatment from a bully. Mention things the student can do to prevent the bullying from getting worse. Collect revised letters and place them in a folder to give the counselor, who will share the letters with students facing bullying.

Sample Letter

Hi Malik,

Today we wrote articles about keeping bullies away. I thought you might want to know one of the tips our group wrote about. We've been friends for a long time. You can tell me it's none of my business, but I saw kids in gym making fun of you because you had trouble shooting a basket.

Why not think of some things you can do before those kids do something worse? You might want to try acting like they're not getting to you. Another thing you can do is try to build up your confidence on the court so you don't get nervous when you play. We can shoot some baskets together at my house for practice.

If I can help, let me know.

Your friend,

Miguel

ACTIVITY 3

Write an Anti-bullying Public Service Announcement

Description: Write and illustrate anti-bully TV or radio announcements to send out your messages to your school. Write a paragraph about the best announcement.

Teaches: Character education (standing up for a cause); persuasive writing about bullying; public speaking skills in delivering anti-bullying messages; and creating posters to reinforce messages.

Helpful Hints:

Talk about how public service announcements on TV and radio make people think about doing positive things, such as achieving in school, wearing seat belts, not drinking and driving, not taking drugs, or staying close as a family.

Discuss how using strong verbs (action words) and visuals (in this case, posters) help make these announcements move people to act in a positive way.

Examples of Strong Verbs

stamp out teasing
combat cruel treatment
fight name calling
crush cyber bullying

Talk about why people often pay attention to short messages more than they do to long ones.

Sample Answer

> People in today's world often prefer short messages because they live faster-paced lives than people did in past generations. People like their messages brief and packed with information. Shorter messages hold their attention and keep them from getting bored.

Discuss the elements of a powerful sentence that will move people to action: a public service announcement contains one main idea that makes good sense; the writers also express their ideas clearly and creatively.

Before small groups present their announcements to the class, remind them of the difference between presenting radio and TV spot announcements. For radio delivery, they will stress expression and speaking clearly. For a TV message, they will emphasize the same things but will add facial expressions and appropriate body language to reinforce their messages.

Entire Class

1. Ask the class to think of public service announcements, brief one or two sentence announcements they've heard on TV or radio.

Examples

"A mind is a horrible thing to waste"
"The children are our future"
"Just say no to drugs"
"Seat belts save lives"

2. Ask why people might pay close attention to such an announcement

Suggested Answers

The announcement is short.
The message is important.
The person saying it seems believable.

3. Have the class generate anti-bullying statements that they will deliver to a TV or radio audience. Write the statements on the board. Have the class vote on the ten best spot announcements and justify their choices.

Small Groups

1. Ask groups or partners to create their own brief announcements (or to choose one that the class composed) about why bullying is wrong:

"Tempted to pick on someone different from you? Celebrate the difference instead."
"Feel the urge to bully? Think twice and walk away."
"You never know where cyber bullying leads. Spread friendship, not hate, on the web."
"Be bigger than the crowd. Don't join in."
"Bystanders save the day."

2. Students will create posters to illustrate their spots. They will deliver their announcements to the class as if they are on TV or radio and will display their posters.

3. You may want to videotape or record the announcements to share with another class. Later, display posters in the halls. Groups will approach the local newspaper or weekly ad paper with their projects and ask if the media would like to print selected announcements.

4. Ask the principal to feature students delivering selected announcements on the public-address system (PA) with the homeroom or morning messages or in an assembly.

Individuals

Students will choose one of the spots that another group presented to the class. They will write a paragraph about why they think the spot announcement they chose will make people think before they hurt someone with words or actions. Students discuss their opinions with the class.

ACTIVITY 4

Know When to Ask for Help

Description: Create wall displays that will inform your classmates about specific times they should tell a parent, teacher, or counselor about a bully. Practice deciding when to tell and not tell. Write a paragraph about telling versus not telling.

Teaches: Using one's intuition and logic to make a decision and learning the difference between telling and tattling.

Helpful Hints:

Ask students to list ways they would tell the difference between bullying and harmless remarks.

Sample Answer

Bullying hurts people's feelings, while harmless remarks are light and silly. Unlike bullying, harmless remarks never involve put-downs or hurtful words. Harmless remarks sometimes come from friends who want you to laugh with them, while bullying comes from someone who doesn't show concern for you as a friend or as a person.

Groups create a display for the classroom or hallway using long sheets of paper. Tell students to use powerful words that strengthen their messages about when to tell or not tell.

Have groups discuss what types of colors and illustration arrangements would reinforce the information in their displays.

Sample Answer

Bright, bold colors and large print would help make the messages meaningful as would arranging similar ideas together to send a coherent message against bullying.

Entire Class

1. Discuss specific instances when it's best to tell a parent, teacher, or counselor about a bully's activities. Have the class also brainstorm situations that they don't need to tell about. Ask how the two types of situations differ. Make a chart on the board. Label one side *Tell* and the other *Don't Tell*. Ask the class to think of at least five examples for each category that they can later use in an individual activity.

Sample Chart

Tell	Don't Tell
A girl tells a classmate that everyone dislikes her, and the whole class starts to ignore her.	A classmate plays an April Fool's Fool's joke on the student sitting next to her.
A boy hits a younger student in the lunchroom because she won't turn over her lunch money.	A student forgets to return a borrowed book to a classmate.
A girl spreads hateful lies about a a classmate on the Internet.	The boy across the street tells you that your dog's an ugly mutt.
A boy constantly trips another student in the lunchroom and calls him *weird* every chance he gets.	Your sister gets hungry and takes the last candy bar.

A group of girls constantly tickles a younger child until she cries.	A girl tells her friend that another student has hairy arms and legs.

2. Stress that the decision to tell or not tell is often an individual judgment call based on how the student feels about the intention of the person making the remarks. Discuss how we can often tell if a person has a hurtful or playful intention.

Possible Answer

Think of the person's past history. Did the person make statements that weren't usually carried out, or did the person do what was spoken about? Has the person bullied other people, and was the bullying severe? Also, consider the person's body language and voice tone. Does he or she sound and look threatening like someone you wouldn't be able to handle on your own?

On the other hand, is the person one who often plays jokes and harmless pranks on classmates? If you have any doubts about whether the person has a hurtful or playful intention, contact an adult and discuss it. It's better to tell and be safe than to take a chance.

3. If there's embarrassment in front of others involved, it may mean that the person experiencing teasing should tell. Ask the class what other things come into play when they have to decide whether to tell or not tell.

4. Ask students to give examples of hurtful words they would need to tell an adult about. Conversely, ask for examples of harmless remarks they've decided not to tell about in the past.

5. Ask the class to discuss the concept of zero tolerance. Under what circumstances should a student never hesitate to tell on a bully?

6. Discuss why children sometimes don't tell an adult about a bully's actions.

Sample Answers

Fear that the bully will retaliate
Embarrassment in front of others
Concern that others will call them *tattletales*

Small Groups

1. Ask small groups to use the ideas the class discussed and their own to create displays about when it's best to tell and not to tell about a bullying episode.

2. As an alternative, some groups may want to create comparison charts about when they should tell or not tell.

3. After groups make their displays or comparison charts, they will explain them to the class and answer questions the class has about them.

4. Have students post displays in the classroom or halls. Ask the principal to have students discuss their best posters (voted on by the class) in a school assembly about bullying.

Individuals

1. Use some of the situations the class thought of for *Tell* or *Don't Tell* (see activity 1, entire class). Ask students to select one of the examples and to write a paragraph about why they think it's a good idea to tell or not tell in that instance.

Sample Paragraph

I believe it's important to tell in the case of the boy who constantly trips a student in the hall and calls him *weird*. Anytime a person hurts someone physically, it's important to tell because it might lead to a serious injury. Also, calling another student names over a period of time can seriously hurt that person's feelings and make the person lose confidence, especially if he or she is shy. Whenever someone hurts another person this way, the person facing this type of bullying should tell because it probably won't stop and may even get worse.

2. Ask students to debate informally their different opinions about when to tell or not tell.

What to Do the First Time a Bully Strikes

Description: Consider how to respond when a bully bothers you for the first time. List verbal put-downs and what you'd say in response.

Teaches: Responding assertively to bullying; deciding when bullying is serious enough to warrant adult intervention; and using effective responses to combat bullying.

Helpful Hints: These activities address the first time one child tries to intimidate another with bullying behavior or makes nasty remarks on a one-time basis. They do not include physical bullying or serious or persistent verbal bullying, which would necessitate immediately informing a responsible adult.

Entire Class

1. Have the class think of things to say and do when a bully makes uncomplimentary remarks for the first time or on a one-time basis. Ask students to think of a bullying situation and have them think of words that would provide a suitable response to a bully.

Examples

One student calls another an uncomplimentary name based on height or weight—the student says: "I don't like you saying that" and walks away.

A student makes fun of another child's clothes—the student says: "I think they're fine" and moves on.

A student calls a special needs student *retarded*—the student says: "Stop saying that" and leaves the scene.

2. Write students' ideas on the board. Have the students vote on the most effective wording; put a star next to the top four ideas.

Small Groups

1. Ask students to think of a time they've seen a bully say something insulting to them or to another child that caught the child by surprise. What words did the bully use, and how did the child respond?

2. Ask them to list what the bully said and what the child said or did in return. Then ask them to think of their own short responses to the insulting behavior.

3. Also, ask the group to decide at what point they should tell an adult instead of handling the problem on their own.

Sample Answers

When they feel they need more support
When the bullying continues or gets worse
When the bullying gets physical or the verbal bullying becomes severe

Individuals

1. Ask students to list five verbal put-downs that a bully might use initially to insult another child. Have the students write at least five sentences that tell how they might react to each put-down.

Examples

Insult

"You can't throw a ball."

Response

"I'm getting better with practice."

"You're really dumb; you know that?   "I think I'm pretty smart, and that's what counts."

"You talk funny."   "That's my accent, and it's part of me."

2. Have students share their ideas with the class. Ask the class to state more responses to counter the verbal put-downs.

ACTIVITY 6

Say What You Mean with Body Language and Words

Description: Groups practice using body language and words to stop a bully. Students list types of body language and speech that will help boost confidence in front of a bully.

Teaches: Character education (self-reliance); confidence in speech and actions; ways to use body language and words to prevent bullying; body language to avoid when near a bully; and deciding which body language techniques work better than others.

Helpful Hints:

Children who are naturally shy may find it difficult to demonstrate some of the body language discussed. Mention that they may want to practice at home so that they will feel more comfortable standing and talking in the ways described.

Discuss how to arrange lists in order of importance. This will help students when they attempt to organize paragraphs.

Entire Class

1. Discuss how the way we stand, gesture, and move makes us appear a certain way to others. Ask the class what people sometimes think of others who walk with their heads down or don't stand up straight

Sample Answers

They don't think these people have confidence.
They're shy.
They're unpopular, and people don't want to be around them.
They're not leaders.

2. What impressions do people often have of those who stand up straight and hold their heads up

Sample Answers

They're proud of themselves.
People look up to them, and they're popular.
They're leaders.

3. Write students' thoughts as they dictate ways that make people appear strong to others

Examples

They stand straight and look up.
They look at people when they talk to them.
They talk loudly enough to be heard.
They look like they know what they're talking about.

4. Ask how these same traits if exaggerated or overdone may cause a problem when talking to others

Examples

Standing straight and tall, if overdone, may make the person you're communicating with fearful.
Staring at someone too hard or too long can make the person feel uncomfortable or threatened.
Talking too loudly can annoy someone.
Looking overly confident might make a person look like a know-it-all.

Small Groups

1. Ask students to think of three different ways they can show confidence through their body language. Ask them to write how appearing strong and confident will make them less likely to be victims of bullying (bullies don't usually bother people who look strong).

2. Have groups demonstrate for the class how they would stand, walk, or talk to help them appear strong and confident. Groups will create short skits depicting a bully making a remark and the victim of bullying using body language that may lessen the bully's power.

Individuals

1. Ask students to make a list of five tips about how to use body language and speech to appear more confident and strong in front of a bully.

Examples

Stand straight and tall.
Keep your head up.
Speak clearly and calmly.
Say what you mean in a few words.
Speak in statements, not questions.

2. Compile a list of all the students' suggestions. Ask the class to tell you which tips they think would help most with a bully.

Think of 10 Ways to Show Kindness to Others

Description: When you feel like saying mean things, try being kind instead. List ten ways to be kind to others and draw pictures that remind you of the ways. Try one of your ideas and later tell the class how it worked. Write ministories about saying or doing mean things versus showing kindness.

Teaches: Character education (consideration and kindness to others); putting ideas about showing kindness to others into practice; using adjectives to describe feelings; and considering the effects of one's actions on others.

Helpful Hints:

Discuss why showing kindness to people may make them feel better than if you said unkind or hurtful things.

Talk about how being unkind may hurt the person acting that way as well as the person being treated unkindly.

Ask students to name ways that others have shown kindness to them and to use adjectives to describe how these words and actions made them feel.

Examples

grateful
content
peaceful
upbeat

Entire Class

1. Ask the class to think of situations in which they felt like responding in a negative way to another child. Then ask them to think of responding to that same child in a kind, positive way.

Examples

Negative Response	Positive Response
"You can't sit with us."	"Sure, you can sit here. There's room for everybody."
"Where did you get those shoes? Nobody wears those anymore.	"Your shoes are different. Where did you get them?"
"You must be dumb if you don't understand that math problem."	"That problem is a little tricky. Can I help you with it?"

1. **Discuss**: Suppose you see someone new at school sitting alone in the lunchroom. How could you make that person feel welcome?

Sample Answers

Ask the person to sit with you and your friends.

Offer the new student help in getting to classes and showing him or her around the school.

Ask the student to tell you about his or her previous neighborhood and school.

2. Ask the class to consider the feelings they would experience if they treated others kindly versus the feelings they would have if they treated someone unkindly.

Sample Answers

positive feelings	happy, proud, and friendly
negative feelings	sad, ashamed, and unfriendly

Small Groups

1. Ask groups to brainstorm at least ten ways to show kindness to others instead of ignoring or saying unkind words.

Sample Answers

Ask someone you've ignored to be on your team.
Compliment another student for a good speech or test grade.
Ask a new student to sit at your lunch table.
Offer to help a student from another country learn your language.

2. Have the groups write their ideas and draw pictures to remind them of the different ways to show kindness.

3. Ask students in each group to put into action at least one of the ways they listed to show kindness to others. Have the groups report back to the entire class in two to four weeks about how they and the person shown kindness felt.

Individuals

1. Write a mini-story (a one page story) in the first person showing a person who feels like treating another child unkindly by ignoring, ridiculing, saying mean words, or hitting. Describe how the person might feel when he or she thinks about treating another person unkindly.

2. Then switch gears and write another mini-story to depict the person showing an act of kindness instead. Tell how that makes the person feel. How will the person receiving the kindness feel? Ask volunteers to discuss contrasting stories with the class.

ACTIVITY 8

Write a Speak-Out Message about How to Stop Bullying

Description: Write a short, dramatic speak-out message about the effects of bullying and how to take action against it. Deliver your message to an audience. Produce a class bully prevention collage.

Teaches: Writing persuasively about bully prevention; learning the difference between fact and opinion; researching bully-related topics; checking the reliability of research sources; and speaking to groups about bullying problems and solutions.

Helpful Hints:

In preparation for the speak-out messages with younger children, you can read short articles or stories about how bullies hurt people and discuss suggestions about bully prevention listed in the articles and stories.

For a homework assignment for younger students, ask parents or homework helpers to find a picture book or chapter book in the library. Ask students to bring their books to school, along with a statement telling how the book taught them something about bullying and how to deal with it.

Choose a few books to read to the class, and ask students to give their statements about the books they brought in.

Ask older students to choose middle grade or young adult novels about bullying; write the titles and authors of the books on the board; and have students read short, interesting excerpts that will motivate the class to read the books.

Also, ask older students to read grade-level appropriate articles from magazines or the Internet and to look at nonfiction books for their age range about bullying. Each group will discuss a specific aspect of bullying and will do their research on that topic. To avoid duplication of topics, approve topics ahead of time. Students will choose topics from a list that the class develops.

Entire Class

1. Explain how to test reliability of sources and to determine if the book, article, or Internet source used as a basis for the speak-out message comes from a reliable person or company. With younger children, explain the importance of the author's knowledge about the subject. Discuss what makes a trustworthy source.

2. Discuss the difference between fact and opinion and why it's important to back up opinion with facts.

Sample Answer

> Fact is proven and tested, while opinion is a person's idea about the way he or she sees things. When you back opinion with facts, it helps a person know that what you're saying is more believable.

3. As students give suggestions for group topics, list them on the board. Ask them to think of more topics than there are groups to give them a wider choice of topics for their speak-out messages. Help younger students break down the topics into subtopics since each group member will give a message on a different aspect of the main topic. Older students will divide the main topic into subtopics when they meet in groups.

Small Groups

1. Students will use the articles and nonfiction books they've read to give a factual basis to their speak-out messages about bullying and how to stop it (Some of the fiction books may also have a factual basis).

2. Every student in the group researches one source and refers to it when delivering an individual three- to five-minute speak-out message on the group topic. The speak-out message is based on fact, and students promote a powerful anti-bully message and solution based on the facts and their own opinions.

Sample Speak-Out Message (3 minutes) for an Upper Elementary or Middle School Class

Everyone needs to get involved in fighting the bullying problem now. This means that parents and everyone in the schools, including teachers, counselors, custodians, bus drivers, and the principal must contribute. The Newark Unified School District in California (Board Study Session, 2007) asks parents to sign an anti-bullying pledge to help stamp out bullying at school.

The school also asks students to sign a pledge to help build a school that honors differences and teaches tolerance. An important part of that pledge states that students will encourage teachers to talk about bullying in class.

I believe that everyone must play a part in fighting bullying. If we see someone hurting another person physically or emotionally, it's important to get involved by saying something to stop it. If we can't handle it alone, we need to tell an adult.

I liked this quote by Albert Einstein in the anti-bullying tips I read on the web: "The world is a dangerous place, not because of those who do evil, but because of those who look on and do nothing." Let's all get together and do something to stop bullying now.

3. Each group hands in a copy of their individual speeches and a list of books, articles, and Internet sources with bibliographical information and a brief summary of each source they consulted to write their speak-out messages. As an alternative, students can list the works they consulted in the body of their speeches.

Individuals

1. Ask the students to state which speak-out message most grabbed their attention and to tell why. Ask them to think of different ways to tell other students about these messages. Have students write one important fact they learned from each group's speak-out message.

2. Ask students to listen carefully to another group's speak-out message that they would like to use to produce a class bully-prevention collage.

3. Ask them to write the messages down when they hear them. Then student volunteers will write the sentences on the collage and illustrate it for a hallway bulletin board.

ACTIVITY 9

Design a Greeting Card with a Positive Message

Description: With your group, create and promote a new greeting card line for children facing bullying. Write and illustrate your own greeting card with a positive message to someone being bullied by another student. Tell how you will support the person.

Teaches: Character education (empathy); speaking to groups; applying fiction and movies to life situations; and using writing and art to encourage someone facing bullying.

Helpful Hints:

Students can give their cards to a child they know who faces bullying. If they don't know anyone personally, they will give their cards to the counselor who will forward them to a student experiencing bullying.

Discuss rhyming and free verse, the two types of verse used in greeting cards. Give students the option of choosing the type and length of verse. Ask why they think shorter or longer verse is better in a card meant to encourage someone who is experiencing bullying.

Ask students to talk about the types of messages they think people would most like to see on this type of card.

Examples

straightforward
sincere
colorful language

What types of illustrations could they draw or cut and paste to reinforce their positive messages?

Possible Answers

nature pictures
friendly animals
stars
pictures of people helping one another

Sample Rhyming Verse for Card

I'm your friend, and I want to say
I hope tomorrow's a better day.
Call me if you need to talk.
We'll play a game or take a walk.

Sample Free Verse for Card

I'm sorry things aren't going well
and that someone is causing you pain.
I'm here for you. Just call or text.
Things will get better in time.

Entire Class

1. Ask the class how hearing encouraging words from family or friends has helped them deal with problem situations in their own lives.

2. Have students discuss fiction they've read or movies they've viewed that show how one person can help another by showing caring behavior.

3. Ask what kinds of feelings students would and would not advise expressing in such a card. Would humor be appropriate in this type of card? If so, what type?

Small Groups

1. Ask students to work together to create a new line of greeting cards directed to children facing bullying. What would they call the new greeting card line? What age group would most likely buy the cards? Ask the groups to make a poster about their new line of cards and to present the line to the class.

2. Have students brainstorm ideas for verses and illustrations to give the class ideas for creating their own individual cards. Tell them to write or remember the best ideas in their groups. After the groups compile ideas, they will report back to the entire class.

Individuals

1. Direct students to create their own greeting cards as a homework assignment. Ask them to design a cover and an inside illustrated message written in free verse or rhyme. Have them sign their first names to the cards.

2. Ask students to read and show their cards to the class. Display all cards before students send them to a friend or present them to the counselor to give to a student who needs encouragement.

ACTIVITY 10

Learn to React in a Flash

Description: Answer the question: "What would you do if? List at least three situations in which it's important to act quickly when a bully bothers you. Think of helpful suggestions to deal with each of the problems. Groups write skits about bullying problems, and the class offers solutions.

Teaches: Knowing when to act quickly against bullying; brainstorming ideas to find solutions; knowing when to seek adult intervention; and expressing opinions in writing and speaking about quick response techniques.

Helpful Hints:

Ask the class to suggest a number of bullying situations that call for immediate action. Write the situations on the board, and have the class number them in order of importance. Leave space next to each situation to record responses to each problem.

Ask the class to give a show of hands for each solution, and leave the three best solutions for each problem on the board.

Discuss why it's important to judge each situation as it comes up rather than having a single solution for each problem.

Sample Answer

Every bullying situation is different even though it may be similar to another you've experienced. While it helps to have some bully prevention techniques to rely on, you need to be sure to fit the one you're using to the situation you're facing.

Entire Class

1. Ask the class to give examples that call for quick action by the person being bullied.

Examples

Another child wants to look at your test paper.
Someone grabs your favorite hat from your head.
Someone threatens to hit you.
A student pushes you in the lunchroom.
A former friend spreads lies about you on the Internet.
A student tells you to hand over your new jacket.

2. Ask the class to give a variety of responses that they think may help keep each problem from escalating. Write these ideas next to the situations as the students dictate.

3. Ask which situations call for immediate adult intervention and which ones the students might try to handle themselves.

Small Groups

1. Have groups write short skits about bullying situations that call for quick action. After each group performs the skit, ask the class what they would do to resolve each problem presented in the skits. Have the class give pros and cons for each solution.

2. Ask groups to act out what they consider the best solution the entire class offers for the bullying situation they presented.

Individuals

Ask students to evaluate the second set of skits they viewed. Which solutions did they find most effective? Which ones did they think wouldn't work? Ask individuals to discuss their ideas with the class.

ACTIVITY 11

Create a Poster Called "You Need to Tell When . . ."

Description: Decide when to tell or not tell about bullying. Write about the times you need to tell an adult about something a bully does. Think about which adult to tell when you need help. Turn your ideas about when it's important to tell into a poster to display in your school or neighborhood.

Teaches: Knowing when to tell; making judgments about the nature of bullying situations; and discussing the validity of different opinions.

Helpful Hints:

Discuss how to make decisions logically (in this case, whether to tell an adult about bullying). What makes a decision a good one for each individual person? Must decisions always be based totally on logic? How can one's instincts about a situation help that person make a good decision?

Discuss telling an adult about another person being hurt by a bully. How can children best do this without putting themselves in danger? Why is it important to help another child facing bullying by telling an adult?

Consider situations where it's best not to tell an adult. How are they different from times it is important to tell?

Discuss the importance of keeping a parent or guardian informed about bullying.

Sample Answer

A parent or guardian knows you best. Your parents should know what's going on at school so that they know when to talk to the teacher, principal, or counselor about the problem.

Entire Class

1. Discuss the difference between telling on someone just to get the person in trouble and telling on the person because bullying creates a harmful situation.

2. Discuss situations in which children should tell without hesitation.

Examples

A child is in physical danger or sees another child facing danger.
Someone is making hurtful and/or abusive remarks.
A child or group of children are using the Internet to spread rumors or to degrade another child.

3 Ask students to list different bullying scenarios. Write them on the board, and ask students to give a show of hands about whether they'd tell an adult or try to handle the situation themselves.

Sample Answers

Tell an Adult

A student says hateful things to you every chance he gets.
Someone steals your lunch money.
A boy in your class kicks you every time you walk by him. A girl calls you unkind names related to your race or nationality.
A group of students threatens to beat you up at the bus stop.

Handle It Yourself

A girl in your class calls you a couple of times and hangs up.
A boy in your neighborhood tells his friends you aren't a good football player.
A girl asks if you got your outfit in a thrift store.
Someone asks to borrow your homework one time.
A girl in your class calls you a *kiss-up* because you get good grades.

---

4. Indicate situations students would tell an adult about with a plus sign and those they wouldn't with a minus sign. Ask them to explain why it is important to tell in each case in which they've listed a plus sign, and why it may not be wise to tell in the instances in which they've listed a minus sign. Have the class debate the advisability of the different answers.

5. Discuss whom to tell (parent, teacher, counselor, principal, or school nurse). What could each of these adults do to help the situation?

Sample Answers

Parent: can provide ongoing support and suggestions to deal with a bullying problem

Teacher: can observe a school bullying problem, talk to the bully about his or her actions, and keep the counselor and principal informed about the problem

Counselor: can listen to the student discuss bullying problems and provide helpful techniques to stop the bully

Principal: can set the tone of the school with a zero tolerance policy on bullying and provide classroom and assembly anti-bully programs

---

Small Groups

1. Each group creates a poster using one of the suggestions that they discussed as a class about when to tell an adult. Have groups choose a situation or assign each group one of the situations so that the groups base their posters on different reasons for telling.

2. Ask groups to follow this format in designing their posters: write one sentence stating, "You need to tell when . . . (write the situation)." Then they will write three to six sentences explaining their rationale for telling in that situation.

Suggested Language to Begin Message

Telling is the best choice because . . .
Telling will help you find a way to stop someone from hurting you . . .
Telling will inform the bully that you won't accept poor treatment . . .
Once someone else supports you, you'll know you're not alone . . .

Sample Answer

You need to tell when someone hurts you physically or verbally in a cruel way that hurts your feelings. Telling is the best choice because no one has the right to harm you this way. Physical bullying can have serious consequences, so you can't let it go on. It's also wise to tell when a bully tries to wear you down with unkind words. Words can hurt as much as hitting.

Telling will inform the bully that you won't accept poor treatment because you know you deserve better. When a bully says things to hurt and embarrass you by abusing you in body or spirit, don't hesitate to tell.

3. Students will illustrate their posters with drawings or cartoons. Display posters in a prominent place in your school. Ask your administrator to have the student body vote on the three posters with the most meaningful messages and to give the winning students small prizes.

Individuals

1. Students make a list of bullying situations they've faced or have seen others experience. They circle the ones they believe they should tell an adult about and write a brief explanation of how they would handle the other ones themselves.

2. Ask volunteers to read their ideas about telling and not telling. The class gives opinions and debates the pros and cons of student responses.

ACTIVITY 12

What Can You Do If Everyone Else Is Bullying Someone?

Description: Is there something else you can do other than join in? Your group will write TV news broadcasts about group bullying and the role of by-standers and perform them for the class. You will also write articles about what you can do if bullying occurs in front of a group.

Teaches: Character education (empathy and taking a stand) and learning how to respond to bullying in a group setting.

Helpful Hints:

Discuss the advantages and problems of speaking out against bullying when a group is involved.

Talk about why it's easier to go along with the crowd rather than stand up for what you believe.

Sample Answer

Many people don't want to go against a crowd because they're afraid the crowd will bother them or make fun of them if they do. They may also be afraid of becoming unpopular with other students. Standing up for what you believe in takes courage and is often a challenge. After you've stood up for someone instead of going along with the crowd, you may find that most kids will agree that helping someone was the right thing to do.

Ask the class to give examples of someone showing courage by taking a stand against something wrong. Have they ever witnessed this in connection with bullying? If so, how did the person help the situation?

Ask the class to discuss why bullies often choose to ridicule others in front of an audience.

Sample Answer

It makes them look big and powerful even though they're not.
It gives them attention in front of others.
It gives them a way to intimidate the children who are watching.

Entire Class

1. Discuss things you can say or do when you see someone being bullied. List different bullying situations (physical abuse, ignoring, and emotional abuse, including hurtful words) on the board as the class suggests them. Next to each situation, as the students dictate, write possible interventions on the part of bystanders.

Sample Answers

Situation	Bystander Response
Hitting, punching, pushing, poking, or hair pulling	Call an adult for help
Ignoring	Tell the bully you don't like what's happening. Invite the person being ignored to be on your team.
Hurtful words	Ask the bully, "Why would you say that?" or "How would you feel if someone said that to you?"

2. Ask the class to evaluate the responses and tell why they would be effective or ineffective in each case.

3. Ask how bystanders can prevent or help stop bullying without putting themselves in danger.

Small Groups

1. Ask groups to discuss the possible consequences of joining in with a crowd that is bullying someone. How would the person witnessing the bullying feel? How would the person being bullied feel? How might a bully behave differently, now or in the future, knowing that everyone in the crowd was not supportive?

2. Each group will write three things a bystander can do or say to counteract what a bully is doing in front of a group.

Sample Answers

Say, "You don't need to do that."

Tell the bullying victim, "Come with us. You don't want to be here," and you and a friend or friends walk away with the bullying victim.

Tell the person bothering someone, "You need to stop now."

Say, "My friend (or friends) and I don't like what you're doing. We want you to stop."

If the bullying gets worse or persists, go to an adult for help.

3. Groups will choose one of their ideas and write a TV news broadcast about a child being bullied in front of others and show how one or more caring witnesses responded to influence the outcome positively.

Individuals

Students will write a brief news article about a person (real or imagined) who has helped stop a bullying situation by taking action against bullying. Post news articles in the classroom and display at parent visitation. Have students send their best articles to the school or local newspaper.

ACTIVITY 13

List 10 Adjectives Describing How a Bullying Victim Feels

Description: Write a mini-story with your group about how a bullying victim might feel years later. Using selected adjectives from your list, you will also write a short fiction story about a child coping with bullying.

Teaches: Character education (understanding the pain bullying causes and the lasting effects of bullying); story writing to promote insight into bullying problems and solutions; and using the media as a writing motivator for bullying issues.

Helpful Hints:

Ask the class to bring in one or more newspaper, magazine, or Internet articles about bullying among children. Read sections of the articles and ask the class to describe how they think the person experiencing bullying feels.

Talk about the difference between fiction and nonfiction and how writers sometimes base fiction on true experiences.

Discuss the short story and how it creates a mood by telling about a single event in a person's life: in this case, bullying. Tell the class that they will try to capture a bullied child's feelings in their stories.

Talk about the advantages of writing in the first person when discussing a problem issue such as bullying (it makes the story more personal, and readers can better understand the person's feelings).

Entire Class

1. Ask students to relate stories about other people (friends, siblings) who were bullied. How did physical or emotional bullying affect them? What emotions did they show or express?

2. Have the class brainstorm a list of ten adjectives that describe how the person felt because of bullying and write the adjectives on the board.

Examples

nervous	angry
scared	excluded
sad	sick
lonely	irritable
depressed	stressful
hurt	embarrassed

3. Ask students which feelings would stand out as those most commonly experienced by a person going through different types of bullying.

Examples

Bullying	Feeling
physical	fear, anger, and nervousness
emotional	sadness, anger, and hurt feelings
ignoring or shunning	loneliness and embarrassment

Small Groups

1. Ask small groups or partners to generate and list ideas for short stories, which they will later write individually. They can base them on experiences they've had or witnessed or on the news stories, articles, or Internet sources they've discussed in class.

2. Have groups take one of the characters and project the person into the future. How might the child feel when he or she looks back upon a bully-

ing experience years later? The group will write a mini-story, and then read it to the class.

Sample Mini-story

Ricardo faced bullying all through grade school because he looked and talked differently from his classmates. When he moved to another state, the students in the middle school there didn't bother him, and he enjoyed the rest of his school years. But he never forgot how he felt when he was bullied in elementary school.

Now that he is an adult with a wife and child, he remembers the names that some of his classmates called him when he first came from another country. He still feels the embarrassment he felt in grade school when the students made fun of him. It is still hard for him to make friends, and it takes a while for him to trust people.

Ricardo told his wife that he would teach his child at an early age how to protect himself against bullying so that he doesn't have to suffer as he did when he was younger. He can't forget what happened, but he has learned from it and will help anyone he sees who faces bullying.

Individuals

1. Ask students to focus on one adjective from the class list (see Entire Class section). They will build their own stories around the feelings that adjective brings to their minds. They can also use the ideas generated by the group.

2. They will write short stories in the first person about a child's experiences with a bully. Ask them to end their stories on a positive note, with the bullying victim beginning to find help with the problem.

3. Distribute the stories to groups and have them choose the five stories they think offer the best depiction of bullying and its effects on a child. Have the students who wrote them read them to the class.

ACTIVITY 14

Keep a Positive Attitude until the Bullying Stops

Description: List positive things you can do to keep upbeat until the bullying stops. Describe how doing these things will help you cope. Design an optimism collage that portrays your action plan. Write a positive e-mail to another student facing bullying.

Teaches: Character education (maintaining optimism in difficult circumstances); helping others cope with bullying; and using literature to explore universal values.

Helpful Hints:

Discuss how keeping positive can help children cope when someone is bullying them. What effect do people's attitudes have on how they deal with problems?

Ask students to consider Viktor Frankl's beliefs in *Man's Search for Meaning*: that it's not so much what happens to us but how we deal with it that counts.

Discuss Frankl's quote: "Everything can be taken from a man but one thing: the last of human freedoms—to choose one's attitude in any given set of circumstances, to choose one's own way." Ask for examples of how this belief would help them in their own life experiences.

The hardest part is waiting for the bullying to let up. Discuss what children can do to keep their spirits up when someone is bothering them. Ask what helps them stay positive when things aren't going right.

Sample Answers

Ask a parent, grandparent, or other relative what they did to keep positive when problems such as bullying struck

Look up quotes such as Frankl's that can help you stay positive, listed by topic in books of quotations on the Internet; and post the quotes in your room to read when you need a boost.

Entire Class

1. Ask the class to list a number of activities they can participate in to maintain good spirits while they're dealing with a bullying problem.

Examples

Helping others
Sports, hobbies, getting together with friends
Relaxation techniques
Exercise
Repeating positive sayings such as affirmations

2. List all of the ideas on the board.

3. Discuss the activities with the class and have students choose their favorite ones. Put a plus sign next to the ideas students think will most help lift their moods when they're facing bullying problems.

4. Explain that groups will design collages, portraying what children facing bullying can do to keep their mood positive. They will write the name of the activity on the collage, explain how it helps promote optimism, and then illustrate their collages.

Small Groups

1. Students will choose one of the activities from the list on the board, using the ones designated by plus signs (Each group chooses a different activity).

2. Ask groups to create a single impression representing their chosen activity with a variety of pictures they'll cut and paste. They can supplement the pictures with their own artwork if they wish.

3. Groups will take turns showing and explaining their optimism collages to the class and will display them throughout the school.

Individuals

1. Students will write an e-mail to another student (real or fictitious) who is experiencing bullying. They will give two suggestions for keeping a positive outlook while the child is dealing with bullying.

Sample E-mail

Hi, Jamal,

   I know some guys are making fun of you and calling you names because you're doing good work at school. Too bad they don't know how important it is to get decent grades. Just want you to know I'm here if you need help. Meanwhile, keep busy doing stuff you like. Here's one idea: maybe we can go see a Piston's game this weekend. My dad has an extra ticket.
   Don't laugh—but how about helping out in the soup kitchen? The people who run it could use an extra hand. It might not be your idea of fun, but it will take your mind off those guys until things ease up.
   OK. Let me know.

Marcus

2. Students will print out their e-mails and exchange them with partners who will pretend they are the people addressed in the e-mail. The receivers of the e-mail will then e-mail the writers of the e-mails back about the advice and how the advice helped them. Volunteers will share their e-mails and responses with the class.

Hold a Contest to Choose the Best Bully-Prevention Poster

Description: Make posters and illustrate them. Write your advice in one sentence and explain it in a short paragraph. Explain why you prefer a certain bully-prevention statement.

Teaches: Displaying helpful bully-prevention material; learning to evaluate bully-prevention advice; discussing bullying with family members; and writing short, striking bully-prevention statements.

Helpful Hints:

Have the class discuss different types of bully prevention advice they've heard or read. What types of advice would be most helpful? What kind of advice would they not offer?

Ask students to discuss bully prevention with their parents or guardians and siblings. Discuss some of their ideas with the class.

Have a student volunteer discuss bully prevention techniques with the school counselor and report back to the class. Ask the class to evaluate the techniques from their own or others' experiences with bullying.

Elicit the principal's cooperation in holding a school-wide bully-prevention poster contest.

Entire Class

1. Ask students to state the best advice anyone ever gave them about dealing with bullying. Discuss the pros and cons of each contribution.

2. Discuss how information from home and school has helped students learn effective bully prevention techniques. If there are any techniques with which they disagree, have them explain.

3. What is the worst advice students have received about stopping bullying? Why do they believe this?

Sample Answer

Beat up the bully, and he or she won't bother you again is not good advice. By retaliating in this way, the bully might strike back even harder. It's best to use tested bully prevention techniques and to talk to an adult if the situation doesn't improve.

Small Groups

1. Students create one or two-sentence bully-prevention statements. Each sentence should employ strong verbs and a forceful message against bullying.

Sample Statements

"Save the day. Stop a bully"
"Arm yourself with bully-busting tips"
"Jump one step ahead of a bully"
"Turn on the power to prevent bullying"

2. After they've discussed and refined their statements, each group chooses one to write on a large poster. Students illustrate the posters with colorful drawings.

3. Students enter their posters in a schoolwide poster contest for the best bully-prevention advice.

Individuals

Students choose one of the bully-prevention statements another group created and write a paragraph explaining why it is good advice and how to carry out the advice most effectively. Students share what they wrote with the class.

Sample Paragraph

I liked "Save the Day. Stop a Bully" because this statement gives a strong message that it's important to get involved when we see a bully doing something to hurt one of our classmates. Bystanders can help stop bullying by taking a stand and saying something. The more kids who speak out to stop the bully, the more power bystanders have to stop someone from being hurt. We can all make someone's day better by getting involved. If the bully is hard to stop or is physically stronger, we can ask an adult for help. The main thing is to take the power away from the bully by helping save the day in any way we can.

LEVEL II ACTIVITIES: INTERMEDIATE

ACTIVITY 16

Be a Caring Bystander

Description: With your group, act out bullying situations in which by-standers are present and consider solutions to these bullying problems. Write about how a bystander helped or hurt a bullying situation.

Teaches: Character education (compassion and personal responsibility); acting out bullying situations that involve bystanders; and learning how to be a helpful bystander.

Helpful Hints:

Tell the students to list bullying situations they've witnessed. Without giving names, students will list bullying situations they've witnessed. You may want to confine incidents they discuss to those that don't involve class members.

Stress the importance of friendship to victims of bullying.

Sample Answers

It helps bullied children feel connected, less helpless and lonely.
It gives them hope that they will eventually conquer the problem.
It makes them feel safer.

Also emphasize that if a bully appears threatening, students must tell a teacher or counselor immediately and in private. In a physically or emotionally dangerous situation, they should not handle the problem themselves.

Entire Class

1. Ask the class to list negative ways they've seen bystanders act when someone is being bullied.

Examples

Laughed at the person being bullied
Joined in making fun of the person
Talked badly about the person
Ignored him or her

2. Ask the class to think of positive things they can do without jeopardizing their own safety when they see a bully bothering another student in a serious way: for example, ask the person privately how you can help; listen to the person being bullied; or tell a trusted adult in private if you feel that the bully could hurt someone.

Small Groups

1. Ask the groups to act out situations in which a child is being bullied. Have each group choose a narrator who will tell the class the circumstances surrounding the bullying.

Examples

The bully asks the child to hand over a pair of new sneakers.
The bully bothers the child who speaks with an accent or looks different.
The bully bothers the child because of a physical or mental handicap.
The bully bothers the child because the child is overweight, underweight, short, or tall.

2. After the groups put on their skits that highlight at least one way bystanders can help a classmate being bullied, the class offers their own solutions.

Individuals

1. Ask students to think of a time they saw another student being bullied and to write what a student bystander said or did to help the situation. (They can fictionalize the situation, using the actual event as a take-off point. They should avoid using names of the people involved).

Sample Answers

a. A group of students teased an underweight classmate in gym class. A girl standing near the group said in a loud, firm voice: "We don't like what you're doing. Stop it now." The students kept making fun of him until one of the girl's friends said, "It's pretty childish to make fun of somebody that never did anything to you." Then everybody watching started cheering the girls on. The teasers must have felt outnumbered because they broke up and left the scene.

b. An older student started punching a younger boy in the playground because the boy wouldn't hand over his video game. Two students walked by and pulled the bully away. He dropped the game at its owner's feet and started running away. Then the boys who helped went to the principal's office and told her what happened. They heard later that she suspended the boy for punching the younger student. The principal wouldn't let him back in school until his parents came in to talk to her about what happened.

2. Have students write one sentence that tells how a student or student bystanders' actions helped or hurt in a bullying situation. The class shares responses.

3. Ask the class to give their ideas about what they would do in some of the situations the students wrote about.

ACTIVITY 17

Produce a Play or Puppet Show about Bullying

Description: Write and act out a short (ten-to-fifteen minute) play or puppet show about bullying for a younger class. Show one child calling another names or bothering or ignoring another child. The person being bullied shows a positive solution to help solve the problem. Write a paragraph about how one skit effectively portrayed a solution to a bullying problem.

Teaches: Examining a variety of anti-bully techniques; observing the effects of bullying in different situations; finding solutions to bullying through drama: and making judgments about the effectiveness of bullying solutions.

Helpful Hints:

Discuss positive and negative solutions to bullying.

Talk about possible themes for anti-bullying skits for a younger audience. Students will choose the grade level and will tailor their subject matter and language level to that group.

If you have a class of younger students, groups will perform their plays for another class of the same grade level or for their own class.

Entire Class

1. Discuss each of the three ways listed that a bully can hurt people: name calling, teasing, or ignoring another child.

2. Ask the class to think of ways to combat these three types of bullying and to discuss how they think the suggestions offered would work.

Sample Answers

Type of Bullying	Ways to Combat Them
Name Calling	Ignore it; use a humorous comeback; and get help if it continues or gets worse.
Teasing	Walk away; stand tall; act and speak with strength; tell the bully to leave; and ask for help if you need it.
Ignoring	Stay with friends who treat you with respect; make more friends by joining more activities; act as if it doesn't bother you; and talk to your counselor about how to deal with it.

3. Discuss the elements of an effective short play; in this case, one written for teaching purposes.

Possible Answers

It gets to the point quickly by showing the problem immediately.
It teaches without being preachy.
It deals with something kids would experience.

Small Groups

1. Students use homemade puppets, dolls, or stuffed animals in the puppet show that takes ten to fifteen minutes to perform.

2. Each group will need a narrator, a head writer who keeps the group focused, a director, and two or more students to play the parts.

3. Ask groups to write discussion questions for the audience and to leave time to answer questions.

Sample Questions

What would you do if a bully bothered you in this way?
What other ways have you seen bullies bother kids in your grade?
What are some other ideas for dealing with the bully in this show?
What was the most important lesson you learned from our show?

Individuals

After groups stage their plays, students will write a paragraph stating which skit they thought most effectively portrayed a positive solution to a bullying problem and explain why. Representative students will read their responses, and the class will discuss them.

ACTIVITY 18

Deal with Family Bullying

Description: Think about the ways children in a family (siblings or cousins) bully each other. Discuss ways to handle bullying within a family. Write a list of *do's* and *don'ts* for living peacefully with relatives. Write about a time you treated a relative unkindly and what you wish you'd done instead.

Teaches: Character education (living peacefully with family members); discussing bullying in a family setting; and experimenting with ways to minimize bullying among relatives.

Helpful Hints:

Ask the class why they think children are more likely to pick on children in their own families.

Sample Answers

ages of children in relation to each other
clashing personalities
competition
jealousy
different temperaments

Discuss what students have done within their own families to stop bullying.

Entire Class

1. Ask students to describe the different types of bullying they've witnessed among children in the same family

Examples

> teasing
> name calling
> physically hurting one another

2. Discuss: How did the child experiencing the bullying react? What made the bullying stop? If it didn't stop, what do they think would help improve the situation?

3. How can parents help put an end to the bullying?

Sample Answers

By not taking sides
By listening when children express concern about the bullying
By setting consequences when one child bullies another

4. When is it important to tell a parent about bullying between family members?

Sample Answer

> You need to tell a parent when the bullying is severe, continues over a period of time, or when it involves physical force.

Small Groups

1. Ask students to brainstorm a list of *dos* and *dont's* for living peacefully with siblings and other younger family members.

Sample Answers

Dos	Don'ts
Treat your relative as you would treat a friend.	Talk to your relative rudely.
Share with your family member.	Be selfish or stingy with your family member.
Honor your family member and show respect.	Use unkind words or physical force with your family member.

2. Have students list their five best *dos* and *don'ts* for getting along with other children in their families. Ask them to print the lists in eye-catching lettering or to use attractive graphics on the computer. Display lists after the presentations.

3. Ask the groups to share their ideas with the class. Have the class discuss the different ideas and comment on their possible effectiveness in a bullying situation.

4. Ask the students to try their ideas with their siblings or other relatives with whom they're having a problem. They will report back to the class on how their ideas are working.

Individuals

Students will write one or two paragraphs about a time they treated a sibling or other relative unkindly and what they might do instead if the situation happened today. Volunteers share their ideas with the class.

Sample Paragraph

One day when my younger sister Jen was about ten, she wanted to play board games with my best friend Lauren and me. I told her to go play with her own friends and not to bother us. She kept begging me to play until I got annoyed. I finally screamed at her and locked her out of my room. It didn't take her long to get the message. That night I heard her crying in her room. I told her I was sorry, but she didn't stop crying for a long time.

If this had happened today, I'd tell Jen she could play one game with us and then she'd have to play with her friends or do something on her own while I visited with my friend. I think that would be a fair way to handle it. I wish I'd treated her kindly instead of treating her rudely. Even though she upsets me at times, she is my sister and I love her.

Write an Imaginary Diary about a Bully

Description: Write an imaginary diary about your experience with a bully. State the problem, how you'll try to stop the problem, and tell what makes the bullying eventually stop.

Teaches: Writing in a diary to find solutions to bullying; writing fiction about bullying based on real life situations; and discussing advantages and disadvantages of bullying solutions.

Helpful Hints:

Discuss the purpose of writing in a diary.

Sample Answers

To record what happens in your life
To tell about something bothering you
To work out problems

Discuss how writing in the first person helps offer insight into a problem.

Sample Answer

First person makes the writing more personal and shows the true feelings of the person writing. Using the first person, *I,* helps the writer get closer to understanding and solving a problem. The writer tells about the problem he or she faced, thinks about it, and tries to come up with solutions.

Talk about someone famous like Ben Franklin who wrote a diary and the things people could still learn today by reading it.

Why do many people like to keep their diaries locked?

Sample Answer

They lock the diary because it is meant only for their eyes. They don't want other people to see their diaries because they contain their most personal thoughts.

When would it be helpful to share what you wrote in a diary with someone?

Sample Answer

If you're having a bullying problem and need to tell a friend or family member, reading your diary account of what happened might help the person understand the problem better. If you just start talking about what happened, you might leave out the important details you'd be more likely to write. When you write what happened, you often include your deepest feelings about the problem. It's totally up to you whether you'd find it more helpful to share what you wrote or to tell the person about it instead.

Entire Class

1. Ask how many students have a diary. How often do they write in it? What kinds of things do they write about? How does having a diary help them? Discuss how keeping a diary might help someone with a bullying problem.

2. Explain that fiction is often based on something the author experienced or read about in the paper. When students write in their diaries, they can base it on a true situation or they can make one up.

3. Ask how changing a real situation to a fiction story can sometimes help a person better understand a situation.

Small Groups

1. Before writing their individual diaries, groups will discuss a variety of bullying scenarios and think of possible solutions that might work in each case. Be sure there are as many situations as there are students in each group.

2. Students in each group will discuss which bullying problem they'll deal with individually in a series of diary entries.

Individuals

1. Students will keep a diary penned by an imaginary bullying victim.

2. Students will write a diary entry at least four times a week for a month. In their first entry they will explain the problem and in the next few entries tell how they are trying to solve it. The last two entries will explain how the bullying eventually stops or how the writer hopes it will stop.

Sample First Diary Entry

Aisha and Cherise, who sit near me on the bus, brought in their pet mice for a science project. They know I'm terrified of mice, but they decided to tease me and to bring their mice into the act. When the bus driver started driving, they opened the cages and let the mice crawl all over my seat.

The beady-eyed rodents scampered on my legs and across my backpack. I started screaming as loud as an ambulance siren, and the bus driver stopped the bus. She called the principal, who gave us all detentions and called our parents to school for a conference.

Sample Final Diary Entry

A couple of days later, after it was all over, I asked a friend to sit near me on the bus for support. I wanted to talk to the girls who had let the mice loose on me.

I explained to them that I didn't like what they did because I was afraid and because it embarrassed me in front of other kids.

I was surprised that those girls actually listened to what I said. But I don't know if other people who do things like this to other kids would do the same. I guess I just had an instinct that they would listen and followed it. I think it's important to do that when you're involved in a bullying situation.

They both apologized and said that even though they were only joking around and didn't think it was a big deal (it was to me), they were sorry I got in trouble because it was their fault. I'm glad we talked about it. They never bothered me again after that.

3. Student volunteers will share their first diary entry, which explains the situation to the class. Then they will tell what they did to solve the problem and read their last two entries.

4. The class discusses the pros and cons of bullying remedies given for the problems listed.

Can People Who Are Different Get Along?

Description: Describe a person who is very different from you in appearance or interests. List ways you can show respect for people who are different. Write a mini-story about a person being bullied because of differences.

Teaches: Character education (appreciating differences); learning ways to show respect to people who are different; and speaking and writing about differences.

Helpful Hints:

Ask students how many ways people can be different from them.

Possible Answers

age
religion
race
appearance

Discuss why people sometimes bully people who are different from them.

Sample Answers

They may feel threatened by people unfamiliar to them.
They haven't learned how to appreciate differences in others.
They may have learned prejudice from others around them.

Entire Class

1. Ask the class to give examples of children experiencing bullying because others see them as different. Ask what happened and how the child reacted to the bullying.

2. Talk about whether the children in the examples could have done anything to stop the bullying. Could anyone else have helped and in what way?

3. Discuss ways to approach differences in a positive way. What can people who are different teach us? How can being friends with those who differ from us help us become better people? In what ways can we be a friend to someone who is different? What should we do if we see someone different from us being bullied?

Small Groups

1. Ask students to list the many ways people can be different and the ways they can be the same.

> **Examples of Differences:** People can be different in weight, height, race, ethnic origin, language, physical and emotional handicaps, age, and interests.
>
> **Examples of Similarities in People:** People can be different yet have similar goals, want the same things in life, have the same feelings and reactions, and enjoy the same activities and hobbies.

2. Discuss what it would be like if we were all the same.

3. Have groups list specific things they can do to show kindness to children dealing with bullying because of differences.

Sample Answers

Talk to them on the playground or in the lunchroom.
Invite them to do something with you and your friends.

If they speak a different language, offer to help them learn yours.
Offer to help with a subject they're having trouble understanding.
Speak out when you see them being bullied.

4. What can people who are different do to get along better?

Sample Answers

Join a school activity.
Invite someone to play a game with you.
Talk to your parents about what's happening at school, both happy and sad
     experiences.
Talk to your counselor about any bullying problems you're having.

5. Ask each group to report their findings to the class.

Individuals

1. Ask students to write a mini-story about a real or fictional person who was
   bullied because he or she was different. Have students answer these questions in the story:

How was the person different?
What did the bully do to hurt the person?
What did the person do to stop the bully?
What did other children do to help the person?

Sample Mini-story

Every day, Lisa and her friend tease Linda, a girl in our class. They make fun of
her because she has a bad complexion and has to go out to the trailer for special help with reading. My friend Melissa and I told Lisa and her friends to stop
teasing her, but they laughed and said, "Maybe we'll start teasing you two instead." Now they've started telling kids in our class lies about Linda, and other
kids are starting to pick on her, too.
     We told Linda to tell the counselor, but she wonders if the girls will get back
at her if she tells. She did agree to go to the counselor if we'd go with her. We've
already set up an appointment, and Linda feels better about it now because she

knows it would be hard to handle on her own. We also told Linda we'd give her ideas for skin care and help her with reading. Linda said she felt better knowing we were on her side.

2. Give each group a few stories and ask them to choose the most interesting story from those they've read. Use numbers instead of names to ensure anonymity. Read these stories to the class and discuss.

ACTIVITY 21

Interview a Relative about a Bullying Experience

Description: Ask an older family member (parent, grandparent, aunt, or uncle) to tell about when someone bullied him or her. What was the situation, and how did your relative react? How was the problem solved? Tell the class your family member's best advice about bullying. Design a poster about your relative's good advice.

Teaches: Character education (intergenerational closeness); discussing bullying with a trusted adult; and sharing family advice about bullying.

Helpful Hints:

Have the class list some things they've learned from an older relative.

Ask why an older relative may be a good person to talk to about a bullying problem.

Sample Answer

An older relative has probably experienced bullying. This person can probably give you wise answers based on experience. It's also important to remember that experts have developed many new techniques since your relative was young. Also, no matter what advice you get about bullying, you have to decide what's best for you. If anyone tells you to hit the bully, think twice about it because the bully might strike back more forcefully.

Entire Class

1. Ask students what types of bullying problems they think were common when their parents or grandparents were growing up. Ask what kinds of bullying problems they observe today that their relatives probably didn't experience. What types of problems are the same?

2. Ask the class to develop questions to ask a mature family member about experiences with bullying. Write the questions on the board and have the students copy them.

Small Groups

1. Have each group choose two questions from the list and three of their own to ask their family members.

2. Each person in the group will write or tape record their family member's answers and report back to the group.

Individuals

1. In addition to having a family member answer the group's questions, each student will ask the relative to give his or her best piece of advice about bullying in one or two sentences.

2. Each student will design a small poster, stating the relative's advice, to post in class. Volunteers will read the relatives' advice to the class, and the class will discuss the advice. Display posters.

ACTIVITY 22

Choose a Fiction Book about Bullying

Description: With your group, write and perform a short play based on a fiction book about bullying and perform it for the class. Write a free verse poem based on one of the plays.

Teaches: Learning to deal with bullying by reading fiction; using books to prompt writing about bullying; writing and performing a play about bullying; and writing poems about solving bullying problems.

Helpful Hints:

Discuss how we can learn ideas that can help us by reading fiction books.

Ask the class to name fiction books they've read about bullying. What did they learn from these books? Make a list of their ideas and add some of your own to distribute to the class.

Entire Class

1. Help the children find fiction books for their age level in the school library, or ask them to go to the library with a family member to choose one. They can choose from among the books on the list you've compiled or find one that appeals to them personally. Students can also look on a search engine for age-appropriate books about bullying. Younger students can ask parents for help.

2. Ask students to give highlights from some of the books they chose and to briefly discuss the plot, theme, and characters.

3. Ask how they think the main character handled the bullying problem. What would they have done in that person's position?

Small Groups

1. Have students in each group choose one of the books they've read (each group chooses a different book) and make up a short play (ten to fifteen minutes) based on the plot and characters of the book. The play should present the bullying problem and what happened to resolve it as shown in the book.

2. Students perform their plays for the class. The class discusses each group's play. Was the solution to the bullying problem one they could use? If they didn't like the author's suggestions, they will explain what they would have done differently.

Individuals

1. Ask students to pretend they are the main character in a book on which one of the groups based their play. They will write a free verse poem about how they felt being bullied and describe how they felt once they began dealing with the problem in a positive manner.

2. Volunteers will read their poems to the class.

Write an Advice Column Letter about a Bullying Problem

Description: Write a letter with your group asking for advice about bullying. Exchange letters with another group and write answers to each other's letters. Afterwards, discuss with the class the different responses each group gave.

Teaches: Responding to letters about bullying problems; writing letters to find answers to bullying problems; and considering different ways of solving the same problem.

Helpful Hints: Talk about the purpose of advice columns with students (Advice columns can help people come up with solutions by featuring problems that are similar to theirs).

Entire Class

1. Ask students to pretend they are asking an advice columnist a question dealing with a bullying problem. Think of a few questions for them to write about.

Suggested Topics for Letters:

Someone in my class tries to steal my lunch.

What can I do to stop him?

A boy in my class calls me "ugly."

What can I say to make him stop?

Some girls are saying mean things   Should I tell?
  about me online.

2. As students dictate questions, write them on the board.

3. At this time, you can also present the following samples as model letters
   for each grade level.

Grade 2

I go to speech class because I have trouble saying certain words. I'm practicing every day, but it's taking more time than I thought. The kids in my class
laugh at me, and it hurts. What can I do to make them stop?
Tongue Tied in Kansas

Grade 3

Nobody wants to play with me at recess. I usually sit on the curb and read.
When I ask someone to play they say, "Don't you have any friends?" or
"Sorry, I can't today." Nobody seems to like me. How can I make friends?
All Alone in Philly

Grade 4

Most of the guys in my class got short haircuts. They say it's cooler when they
play sports. Now they're starting to tease me and call me a *girl* because I
wear my hair longer than they do. I screamed at them and told them to stop,
but things got worse. How should I handle this?
One of a Kind in Ohio

Grade 5

The girls in my class are starting to look more mature, and I still look like
a little girl. My mom doesn't help because she won't let me wear the cute
styles the other girls wear, and she makes me keep my hair short, not long
and silky, like the other girls wear theirs. Now some girls from the popular
crowd are starting to make fun of me and call me *baby*. Can you help me?
Little Miss in Mississippi

Grade 6

My friends' parents drop them off at the mall every Friday night. I'm not al-
lowed to go because my parents say it's not safe and that I might get in trou-

ble. Now some of my friends don't want to hang out with me and say I'm no fun. They've stopped inviting me to their sleepovers and parties. I want my friends back, but I'm sick of how they're acting.
Overprotected in Ohio

Grade 7

My older brother and his friends tease me because I don't have muscles like they do. They call me names like *wimp* and *scrawny*. Once my brother punched me to "toughen me up." I'm starting to feel nervous that he and his friends might rough me up badly, but I'm afraid to tell. Please answer soon.
Shaking in LA

Grade 8

I'm on the school bowling team, but I always get the lowest score. I like bowling, but I've always been shy, and I freeze when it's time to roll the ball down the alley. Because I get nervous, I usually drag down the team's score. A couple of kids on the team have started calling me "gutter ball" and rolled their eyes when I got up to play. I hated when they embarrassed me, so I dropped out of the team. Now they're still teasing me, and other kids are joining in. What should I do?
Losing in Las Vegas

Small Groups

1. Have each group make up a question, geared to their age group, asking advice about a bullying problem. You can use any of the above examples for different age groups, depending on the interests and maturity of your class.

2. Ask the groups to exchange questions with another group and to answer another group's question in a letter to a fictitious person being bullied.

3. Ask the groups writing the letters to give the answers back to the group that wrote the letter.

4.. Have students read their letters and answers to the letters aloud, and have the class discuss the advice given for each question.

5. Allow time for the class to comment on the replies.

Here is a sample letter with a response:

Sample Advice Letter

Dear Advice Guru:

I'm an average-looking girl, somewhat overweight, who gets good grades and loves sports, especially softball. I have a couple of good friends and get along with most of the kids in our class, but I don't belong to a group.

Lately, a boy in my class has been calling me *ugly* and other mean names every chance he gets. Last week in assembly he sat in back of me and kicked my seat, pushing me forward. My back ached all afternoon. I didn't appreciate his doing that and I told him so, but he just laughed.

Before he started bugging me, I heard that a girl in my class told him I liked him, which is definitely not true. Maybe he doesn't want anybody to think he'd ever be seen with me, and that's why he acted this way. I don't care why he's doing it. I just want him to leave me alone. How can I get him to stop bugging me?

Hurt feelings in Ocean City, NJ

Sample Response Letter

Dear Hurt,

Don't accept the treatment this student gives you. Not only does he continue to call you names, but he also hurt you physically, which is serious and unacceptable.

Be sure to talk to your parents and let them know what he's doing.

Also, try talking to your teacher or counselor. Tell them how you've tried to stop him from bothering you, and explain how the bullying continues.

Stay close to your friends. And above all, believe that this will end someday.

Sincerely,

The Advice Guru

Individuals

Ask students to write about the best advice given by one of the groups and to explain why they would try the idea.

Imagine You're a News Team Reporting a Bullying Episode

Description: Your group imagines it's a news team reporting on a bullying episode that happened at a local school. Give a special report about a bullying episode, and send out a message about how big a problem bullying is today. Write and discuss your opinions about bullying as a major problem in schools and neighborhoods.

Teaches: Learning about the media's role in promoting bully prevention and understanding the roles of different people in handling bullying problems.

Helpful Hints:

Talk about how a news team gives a report on a current issue, using more than one reporter to investigate different parts of the same story.

Discuss how the media makes people aware of problems, such as bullying. Ask the class to discuss different issues reporters (both print and TV) have brought to the public's attention, causing people to take action.

Entire Class

1. Ask the class to think of a serious bullying episode that happened or could happen at school.

2. Discuss how the children think the person being bullied might handle the situation; what the teacher or principal would do; and what the adults at school could do to prevent it from happening again.

Small Groups

1. Ask the students to imagine they're on a TV news team. What kinds of questions would they ask the different people involved in a bullying situation? Make a list of questions they would ask the teacher, principal, bystanders, and the bullies.

Sample Questions for Teachers: What types of bullying do you see in your classroom and in the school? What do you think a child facing bullying should do to stop each type of bullying you've listed? What works best to prevent bullying? What is one thing you as a teacher can do to help prevent bullying?

Sample Questions for the Principal: Do you have a bully-prevention program in your school? What kinds of things does your school do to stop bullying problems? What is the best advice you can give someone facing bullying?

Sample Questions for Bystanders: What did you do when you saw a student bullying someone? How did you help the person being bullied? How did the bully react when you got involved? What plan do you have for stopping bullying the next time you see it? What advice would you give someone witnessing a bullying episode?

Sample Questions for Bullies: How do you think you'd react if a bully bothered you? How does bullying make you feel about yourself and about the person being bullied? What plan do you have to stop bullying other children in the future?

---

2. Ask students to incorporate answers to these questions in their newscasts when they work in their groups.

3. Ask groups to start out by talking to their TV audience about bullying as a major problem among children today. In making their report as a news team, ask groups to consider what happened to the person being bullied;

whether anyone could have prevented the mistreatment of this student; and what the victim might have done to prevent or stop the bullying.

4. Each news team member reports to the class on a different aspect of the incident.

5. You may want to videotape the news broadcasts to show to other classes.

Individuals

Based on the newscasts the groups present, students write and discuss their opinions about bullying as a major problem in schools and neighborhoods.

What If a Bully Wants Something You Have?

Description: Does the person bothering you want a video game, sports equipment, clothes, or homework? With your group, role-play situations in which someone demands something that you own. Write a paragraph about why your ideas are as important as your personal property. Write some things to say to someone who asks you to give away your ideas.

Teaches: Understanding how ideas are also property; finding solutions to bullying that involve demanding personal property; and giving effective answers to someone who demands personal property.

Helpful Hints:

Discuss: What is the difference between sharing willingly and having someone force you to give up something important to you?

Ask the class how they feel when they share versus when someone demands something from them.

Entire Class

1. Have students discuss situations in which someone has tried to force them to give up something that belongs to them. List them on the board.

2. Ask the class to think of effective responses for each situation and to list them next to each situation. When would a child need an adult to assist

in any of these situations? Place a check mark next to these situations as students list them.

Sample Answers

Situation	Response
A student demands a baseball glove from someone on the playground.	The glove's owner says, "You're not taking this," and walks away.
A student asks a classmate if she can copy her homework.	The classmate refuses but says, "If you need help, I'll work on it with you."
In the bathroom, a student punches someone from his neighborhood because he thinks the boy said something bad about him.	The student who is attacked reports the incident to his counselor.

Small Groups

1. Each group will role-play two of the situations listed on the board in which one child demands something that belongs to another. They will use props (an item of clothing, homework, etc.) and reenact a bullying episode. They may want to provide bystanders and school staff in their plays.

2. Students will use the ways suggested in the class discussion to respond or may use another technique their group prefers.

Individuals

1. Students will write a paragraph stating why they think ideas (test answers or homework) hold as much, if not more, importance as material possessions, such as clothes and toys.

Sample Paragraph

I think ideas such as test answers, homework, or reports are personal property like my sports equipment and clothes. In fact, my ideas are more important than other things I own because they come from my brain, and I worked hard to create them. I use my ideas to help me pass a test, do homework, and to write reports. Why should I let someone steal them when I've done all the work?

2. Students will also write at least three responses they can give if someone asks for their test answers, homework, or report. Discuss with the entire class.

Sample Responses

Test Answers   I can ignore the person or shake my head *no*.

Homework   I can say that I spent a lot of time doing it and that I don't want to give it away.

Report   I can tell the person to do his or her own work, or I can offer to help but not do the report.

What If Someone Bullies Someone Who's Not a Close Friend?

Description: You don't like to see someone bullying another child, but you're not a close friend. How can you help the person? What can you say or do? With your group, write a poem about helping someone you don't know well. List things you can do to help children who aren't close friends.

Teaches: Character education (seeking advice from relatives); deciding when to get involved; thinking of ways to help stop bullying in schools and neighborhoods; and writing and reading poems about helping others.

Helpful Hints: Ask students to discuss with parents or other older relatives an event in history or in their own lives when someone got involved in another person's problem. Have students discuss with their relatives why they got involved and how the problem was helped or eliminated. Have students report on their conversations with a family member to the class.

Entire Class

1. Ask students to talk about a time a person got bullied and they saw strangers trying to help. What did the people who didn't seem like close friends do to help? How did it work?

2. Ask what types of precautions children should take when trying to help a stranger so that they don't put themselves in danger.

Small Groups

1. Ask groups to tell why it's important to help someone even if they don't know him or her personally. Have them report to the class about how someone has helped them in a bullying situation or how they have helped someone.

2. Have groups write and present a poem about why helping another person being bullied is important to the person, to himself or herself, and to the world.

Sample Poem

Try saying something
when you see someone
teasing, hitting, or
talking about another person
in a cutting way.
Say, "Stop," or "You
don't need to do that."
Tell a grown up
if things get worse or continue.
Say something to help someone
and to help create a better world.

Individuals

Ask students to make a list of ways they can help children they don't know personally deal with bullying. How can they play a part in stamping out bullying in school and in their neighborhoods? Students discuss their ideas with the class.

Sample List

Ask the child how you can help.
Listen to the child and ask if he or she wants to talk.
You and a friend or friends tell the bully that you don't like what's going on.
Rescue the person being bullied by inviting him or her to join you and your
    friends.
Ask the counselor to help you and your friends start a bully prevention club.

How Can Having Friends Help with Bullying?

Description: Why is it important to have friends you can count on? With your group, list ways to help a person make friends. Interpret and discuss quotes about friendship.

Teaches: Discussing the importance of friendship; sharing ideas for making friends; discussing how friends can help with bullying; and interpreting and applying quotes about friendship.

Helpful Hints:

Some people make friends more easily than others. Discuss why some children might find it hard to make friends.

Have the class discuss how people who have few or no friends may face more problems with bullying than those who do.

Sample Answer

Bullies tend to bother loners; those with few or no friends don't have a support system when they face bullying problems; and these children have no one to confide in when they experience problems with other children.

Entire Class

1. Discuss why having friends is important. Ask the class what friendship means to them.

2. Ask students how having friends has helped them if they had a problem with bullying.

Sample Answer

> Friends can help by staying close by when a bully causes a problem; they can listen sympathetically and offer suggestions if a bully bothers you; and they can help you stay hopeful until the bullying stops.

Small Groups

1. Ask groups to discuss the main qualities they look for in a friend. Ask them to think of ten ways a person can make friends.

Sample Answers

Join school clubs; volunteer at school.
Offer to help someone with a school subject.
Offer to teach someone a sport or skill.
Start a conversation with someone you'd like to have as a friend.

2. After completing their lists, students will narrow their lists down to what they consider the five best ways to make friends.

3. Suppose making friends is hard for someone. Ask groups to think of what that person can do to make a friend and to add it to their five best ways to build new friendships.

4. Have the groups consider how having friends can help someone facing bullying. Groups discuss their ideas with the class.

Individuals

1. Students will write their interpretations for any two of the following quotes about friendship:

---

a. "The only way to have a friend is to be one."
(Ralph Waldo Emerson)

Sample Interpretation: It's important to show your friends that you care about them by being a good listener and by standing by them when they need your help. If you're a good friend, your friends will usually stand by you and treat you like the friend you are to them.

b. "One who looks for a friend with no faults will have none."
(Hasidic Saying)

Sample Interpretation: Everyone has faults. As friends, we need to over-look faults and concentrate on our friends' good points. It's important to accept our friends for who they are just as they accept us in spite of our faults.

c. "Friends are the Bacon Bits in the Salad Bowl of Life."
(Pizza Place Sign)

Sample Interpretation: Good friends add an interesting ingredient to our lives. They make every day seem brighter and more interesting. Good friends spice up our lives just as bacon bits make a salad more delicious.

d. "My best friend is the one who brings out the best in me."
(Henry Ford)

Sample Interpretation: We always want to be at our best for friends because they do everything they can to make our lives happier. We see everything differently, in a more positive way, because of the joy our friends bring us. They make us better people.

---

2 Ask the class to share their interpretations and to tell how they can apply these quotes about friendship to their lives.

3 For extra credit, some students may want to find and discuss their own quotes about friendship.

Be a Good Listener to a Person Being Bullied

Description: Help someone deal with bullying by really listening to that person. With your group, stage a short skit showing a child discussing a bullying problem with a good listener. Write a character sketch about a good listener.

Teaches: Character education (showing concern for others by listening); how to be a good listener by using body language and speech; dealing with bullying problems with the help of a good listener; and using listening skills to help others.

Helpful Hints:

Discuss what makes a good listener.

Ask the class to explain how they told a good listener about a problem and how the person helped.

Entire Class

1. Tell the class to think of things they can say and body language they can use to listen to someone who has a problem.

Examples

Don't hurry the person you're listening to.
Have good eye contact.

Nod or use other gestures to show you understand and are paying attention. Listen to the person talking rather than talking about what happened to you.

2. Have students describe how they feel when someone really listens to them versus when someone doesn't listen.

3. Discuss why listening is often more important than talking when someone has a problem.

Sample Answer

When people have problems, they want us to listen and not talk too much because they first want us to understand the problem. If we're talking, we're not hearing the other person but giving our own ideas based on what we, not the person, thinks. Listening is also more important than talking because it gives the person with a problem a chance to put feelings into words, to think about a problem, and, hopefully, to solve the problem by coming to his or her own conclusions.

Small Groups

1. Groups compose and perform short skits showing a child telling a good listener about a bullying problem.

2. Groups dramatize how the listener helps the person with the problem.

3. The class comments about each skit, saying how the listener helped the person with a bullying problem.

Individuals

Write a character sketch about the best listener you've ever met. What makes the person a good listener? What did you learn from that person, and how can you use what they taught you with others? Selected students read their descriptions to the class.

Sample Character Sketch

Hope, my older sister, is the best listener I know. She always gives me as much time as I need to discuss a problem. She never makes me feel rushed by looking as if she's thinking of something else.

If I tell her a problem, she looks at me when I'm talking and says things that make me know she understands, such as, "Tell me more," or "How did that make you feel?"

She also asks me what I think I can do to solve the problem and tells me that I can always count on her if I need help. Hope listens and never judges me or makes me feel like I'm the younger sister. I've always felt that we're complete equals and best friends. I hope I can help someone by being a good listener as my sister has helped me.

ACTIVITY 29

How Can Body Language Help or Hurt a Bullying Situation?

Description: Learn ways that body language can help or worsen a bullying situation. Write skits showing positive and negative body language and facial expressions. Draw pictures of effective and ineffective facial expressions to use with bullies.

Teaches: Learning the importance of body language in keeping bullies away; differentiating between helpful and unhelpful facial expressions to use with bullies; and knowing the difference between positive and negative body language.

Helpful Hints:

The way we use body language can help or hurt a bullying situation.

Ask students why the way they react to a bully without using words can improve or hurt the situation.

Ask the class to name times when making certain facial expressions or using body language has helped or hurt them in interacting with others.

Sample Answers

BODY LANGUAGE THAT HELPED

When I stood up straight and tall to give a speech in assembly, my friend said I looked like I had confidence.

When I smiled at a new girl and welcomed her to our school, she said she was glad to see a friendly face.

When I looked in my cousin's eyes and tilted my head when she told me her problem, she said I was a good listener.

BODY LANGUAGE THAT HURT

When I raised my eyebrow at something a friend said, she thought I was being sarcastic.

When I rolled my eyes when my mom asked me to do something, she thought I was being disrespectful.

When I slouched in my seat so my teacher wouldn't call on me, he thought I didn't study and wasn't prepared.

Entire Class

1. Ask the class to name different types of body language that may worsen or help calm a bullying episode. Label two columns on the board *help* and *hurt*. List students' ideas under each column.

Sample Answers

Help	Hurt
Stand straight and tall. Speak with strength and confidence.	Slouch and look at the ground.
Speak in short sentences, using statements.	Speak in long sentences, using an unsure, questioning tone to end sentences.
Keep your expression neutral so that the bully doesn't know what you're thinking and doesn't react strongly.	Laugh at the bully or look frightened.

2. Discuss why using positive body language may not always work during a bullying episode.

Sample Answers

Bullies often don't pay attention to their victim's reactions; sometimes bullying happens so fast that a child may not have a chance to decide how to react; and sometimes a bully may misinterpret a person's body language.

Small Groups

1. Have groups write mini-skits (about five minutes each) showing a bullying encounter between two children. Then show the person being bullied in the same scenario, first responding with positive, strong body language and facial expressions (strong expression and stance and firm but non-threatening expression), and then with negative body language (laughing or smirking) or weak (shoulders slumped or looking downward) body language.

2. Ask the class to comment on both types of body language used and to tell why they think one was more effective than the other in deterring the bully.

Individuals

1. Ask students on one side of the room to draw a face that shows an effective facial expression to use in a bullying situation. They will label the lips, eyes, and eyebrows with descriptive phrases that explain why certain expressions may help ward off a bully.

2. Students on the other side of the room will draw faces that show facial expressions that won't help a bullying situation. They will also label and explain parts of the face involved to show why certain expressions may not work.

3. Ask a few students to show and explain their drawings to the class.

ACTIVITY 30

Act Out Humorous Things to Say If a Bully Teases You

Description: With your group, think of something a bully might say to tease someone, and act it out. Think of some funny things you might say to lighten things up without insulting the bully. Compare them to replies that might make the situation worse. Write a comic strip showing a teasing incident and how you might effectively respond.

Teaches: Using humor to diffuse teasing; considering boundaries in using humor to stop teasing; and practicing humorous responses to teasing.

Helpful Hints:

Discuss: How can you use humor to put a teaser off guard?

Ask the class how telling a joke can sometimes help a tense situation.

What kind of humor is never good to use with a teaser?

Entire Class

1. Ask the class to describe a teasing incident they've witnessed. What humorous thing could the person have said in each situation to make the teaser stop and think? Would making a joke be the right thing to do in each situation? Explain.

115

Examples

Teasing Incident	Humorous Thing to Say
1. Your big, bulging eyes make you look like an alien.	That's OK. I see more that way.
2. Where did you get those weird shoes?	I got them at a costume store for clowns.
3. Your arms and legs are hairier than a gorilla's.	Some of my best friends live in the zoo.
4. Your hair looks like a grease pit.	I save water by washing it every other day.

Ask the class to give examples of what they wouldn't say to a teaser in each of the situations given and to tell how these words might backfire.

Examples of What Not to Say:
(Refer to the numbers of the teasing incident examples listed above.)

1. "It's better than having rat eyes like yours."
2. "I bought my shoes at the same place you bought yours, the dollar store."
3. "That's not as bad as having a gorilla face like yours."
4. "I wish you'd get stuck in a grease pit."

All of these responses to a teaser might backfire because they could provoke the teaser to bother a person more, or even to use physical force against the person. Humor works better than the sarcasm used in the first three examples and the anger used in the last one.

When you use humor against a bully, consider, first of all, whom you're talking to. Can the person take a joke, or is he or she the type of person you shouldn't respond to at all? If the bully seems like the type who would ease up after the joke, be sure the joke is light and silly, not cutting and heavy like the ones above, or the bully may come back at you more forcefully.

---

2. Discuss why it's never a good idea to insult the bully. How could you cross the line in responding to a teaser? What might happen if you went beyond those limits?

Small Groups

1. Have groups make up short scenes (about five minutes each) that show examples of teasing incidents. They will come back with a funny response that works and one they think won't work.

2. After each scene, ask the class to tell why one humorous response might work and the other probably would not.

Individuals

1. Ask students to draw comic strips (with two pictures) depicting one child teasing another. The child being teased comes back with a funny saying. Ask students to depict the teaser's reaction to the joke.

2. Have them write one sentence telling why they think their humorous response would help stop the teasing. Post comic strips around the room.

ACTIVITY 31

Write an Anti-bullying Song or Rap

Description: With your group, write a song or rap to put out the word against bullying in any form. Perform your song or rap for the class. Write an opinion paragraph about your favorite song or rap.

Teaches: Using music to spread an anti-bullying message throughout the school and discussing anti-bullying ideas with family members.

Helpful Hints: Discuss: Why is bullying wrong? What can we do to stop bullying? Ask the class to think of key phrases and sentences that will help spread the word against bullying behavior. Write the phrases and sentences on the board.

Entire Class

1. Ask students to discuss with their family ways that music helps influence people to do things.

Example

Commercials and popular music with positive messages.

Students report back to the class about their discussions.

2. Discuss what makes a good song or rap to promote an idea

Sample Answer

Short, clear message delivered with expression and a memorable melody.

Small Groups

1. Ask groups to use the phrases and sentences on the board (see helpful hints) to develop a anti-bullying song or rap lyric. Groups will write a short lyric and a refrain they will use at the beginning and end of the lyric. They can use original music, a melody they've heard before, or they can recite the rap.

Example

Recited Rap

We are the bully busters
and we're here to say,
"You've got the power
to stop a bully today."
There are lots of things
that you can do
to keep the bully at bay.
Look tall, stand tall,
Know what to say
to make the bully go away.
If that doesn't work,
get help right away.
Stay strong, don't give up,
and you'll see a brighter day.

Refrain

We are the bully busters
and we're here to say,
"You've got the power
to stop a bully today."

2. Selected groups perform songs or raps for the entire class or for other classes (Some students may want to use their own instruments). Display lyrics throughout the building and hold a schoolwide contest to vote on the best song lyric. The best act, as determined by peers, can perform in a school assembly.

Individuals

Ask students to write a short opinion paragraph about one song or rap they've heard from the groups that they'd use to spread the word about bullying. How did the words and melody work together to build a message to stop bullying? Students discuss opinions with the class.

LEVEL III ACTIVITIES: ADVANCED

ACTIVITY 32

Design a Handbill to Teach about Bullying

Description: Design a handbill about bullying to give to other kids. In the handbill, point out things a bully does to bother other children and list specific ideas to combat each problem. Distribute handbills throughout the school.

Teaches: Character education (offering encouragement to others dealing with bullying); finding practical solutions to bullying problems; choosing the best anti-bullying solutions, and writing and disseminating anti-bullying information.

Helpful Hints:

Explain why people give out handbills, small papers with important messages.

Sample Answer

To explain an idea to others and to get the word out about something important, such as bullying, to other students.

Ask why a handbill would be a good tool to give children tips to use if they're bullied

Sample Answer

Children can read it quickly, learn something new about bullying, and pass it on to another person.

Entire Class

1. Make a chart on the board. Label one side *Things a Bully Does* and the other, *Things I Can Do*. Ask the class to brainstorm ideas about things a bully does to bother people. Make a list of these things under the first heading.

2. Have the class think of ideas to deal with each form of bullying; write the ideas on the board next to the corresponding item in the second column, *Things I Can Do*.

Examples

Things a Bully Does	Things I Can Do
Asks for a test answer.	Ignore the student or say *no*.
Hits me on the back.	Tell an adult I trust.
Tells me my clothes are ugly.	Walk away or come back with something like "Thanks for noticing."

3. Ask the class to review the list in the second column and to choose the five best ideas for dealing with each type of bullying.

Small Groups

1. Tell groups to design handbills, cutting a standard size white or tinted paper horizontally into two pieces.

2. Each group should think of a theme for the handbills their groups will create. Here are some examples:

> The Bully Did What?
> What Bullies Do, What I Can Do?
> Beating Bullies at their Own Game

3. Using the *Things a Bully Does* and *Things I Can Do* format that the class developed, each group member writes three ideas on a separate handbill. They may consult group members to gather ideas and to determine which ideas the group likes best.

4. Group members will write the theme statement that their group chose on the top of their individual handbills. They will illustrate their handbills with colorful lettering to make them visually appealing. Group members may help one another with illustrations.

5. Students discuss the information on their handbills and display them in the classroom.

6. Ask a student from each group to donate his or her handbill to the counselor, who will use them with students trying to cope with bullying.

Individuals

1. Have students write the three best tips they've heard from the groups and tell why they think these tips would work well.

2. Students distribute their handbills to others at recess and in the cafeteria, explaining that they're involved in a class project on bullying.

Plan Panel Discussions about Bullying

Description: With your group, research books, magazines, and the Internet in preparation for panel discussions about bullying. Write your opinions about one of the discussion topics.

Teaches: Researching bullying solutions with a variety of sources; staging panel discussions to enlighten classmates about bullying; logically organizing research material; and using panel discussions as a springboard for independent learning about bullying.

Helpful Hints:

Explain how panel discussions help enlighten people about different aspects of a topic and how TV and radio journalists use them to give information about an important topic.

Discuss how to use research to find information about bullying problems and possible solutions. Ask the school librarian to speak to the class about finding books, magazine articles, and web resources for children about bullying (Parents can help younger students look up and document research for panel discussions).

Entire Class

1. Ask the class to think of different topics that fall under the banner of bullying. Write them on the board and have students generate four to six

subtopics for each of these main ideas. Have them think of a few extra topics so that groups have a wider choice for panel discussion topics. Give practice in arranging the subtopics in a logical order.

2. Be sure that the topics cover different areas of bullying even though they may overlap.

Examples

Best bully prevention tips
Girl versus boy bullying
Common bullying problems in our school
Why people bully
When to tell
Bullying in the family
Bullying outside of school
Internet bullying.

Small Groups

1. Ask individual students in the group to prepare a separate section of the panel discussion based on at least two sources they have researched. Each student will speak for at least five minutes on one aspect of the topic.

2. After the panels present their findings (a mixture of facts and opinions), allow time for a brief question-and-answer period. Students hand in a brief summary of their research sources (Younger students can hand in a list of sources developed with a parent's help).

3. Ask the class to write at least two facts they learned from each panel discussion and to hand them in.

Individuals

1. Have students write their opinions about one of the topics addressed by the groups. Why did they find it an important topic? What was the main

point the group made about it? What more would they like to know? What original ideas can they add to the topic? Discuss.

2. Ask volunteers to further research the topic that interests them and to report back to the class.

ACTIVITY 34

Debate What It Means to Join a Clique or Crowd

Description: Look up the meaning of *clique* in the dictionary. If you belong to a clique or crowd, tell about the good points and bad points. How can cliques cause problems for kids who don't belong? How can they cause problems for members? With your group, debate the pros and cons of belonging to a crowd. Write an opinion essay about joining versus not joining a crowd.

Teaches: Debating the positives and negatives of joining a crowd; using family as a resource to study bullying; and writing opinion essays about cliques and crowds versus having friends from different groups.

Helpful Hints:

Ask the class to define what it means to belong to a clique or crowd as opposed to having friends from different groups.

Ask class members to discuss with one or more relatives the positive and negative aspects of belonging to a clique or exclusive group. They can ask the family members whether they liked belonging to one group or if they preferred having friends from different groups. What were the advantages and disadvantages of their choices? Hold a class discussion about the class's findings.

Sample Answers: Positives and Negatives
of Belonging to a Group

Positive

Negative

Friends are always around. You see the same familiar faces every day.

You may have little time alone. You're limited to one group and don't get a chance to meet other people.

You always have something to do because the group is always doing things together.

Sometimes you want to do your own thing and not be a part of the group.

Entire Class

1. Ask the class to list from their own experiences the positive and negative points of belonging to a crowd. Write ideas on the board. Discuss why many children want to be part of a group. Is it possible to belong to a group but also to make room for other friendships?

2. Discuss what it feels like not to be part of a group. Can a person be happy without having a special group of friends?

Small Groups

1. Explain that a formal debate has certain rules. Although students will discuss the pros and cons of joining a crowd, they will debate it in a more informal manner by stating their positions and backing them up with facts and opinions.

2. For purposes of the group debates, arrange students in equal numbers so that one side agrees with the benefits of joining a crowd and the other doesn't.

3. After groups stage their debates, the class votes on which side won for each group, and volunteers explain why they voted a certain way.

Individuals

Students write an opinion essay telling why they choose to belong to a crowd or have many friends. What benefits do they receive from their choices? If they would rather not be in a crowd but would rather maintain friendships with children from different groups, have them explain why they chose that path. Students discuss their choices with the class.

Sample Opinion Essay 1
Why I Belong to a Crowd

I like having one group of friends I can depend on. We all share the same interests, such as movies, shopping, and wearing the same kinds of clothes. Other kids know right away we're in the same crowd because we all look, act, and talk alike.

We enjoy our time together, but I have to admit that sometimes I'd like to be friends with some other kids in my class although I'm not sure the group would accept them. Also, I don't want to take the chance of getting anyone in the group angry with me because they might not want me to be in the group anymore.

Sample Opinion Essay 2
Why I Don't Belong to a Crowd

I'd rather have many friends and not belong to a crowd because I enjoy knowing many different types of people. I also don't like going along with a crowd in the way I dress or in the things I like to do. I'm friendly with some guys who play football like I do, but I also like drama club and see some of those kids on the weekends.

I feel that it's not good to tie yourself down with one group of kids when you can have a lot of friends with different ideas and interests. Sure, sometimes I miss the comfortable feeling of having one group of friends, but I like my independence more.

Write an Acrostic Poem about Bullying

Description: Small groups or partners write a poem using the first letters of a word or words related to a bullying problem or solution. Write the word or words in a column. Use the word to write a poem. For example, use the first letters of words such as *teasing* or two words, such as *stand tall,* to write each line of the poem.

Teaches: Using poetry to spread the word about bullying and choosing the best ideas for bully prevention posters.

Helpful Hints:

Students will choose one or two words on which to base their acrostic poems. Ask them to try using phrases (parts of sentences rather than complete sentences) for the first few words of their poems and a sentence to end it.

Explain how an acrostic poem uses the first letters of words or sentences to design a poem. Here's an acrostic poem using the word *friend*:

> Faithful and caring
> Right there when you're needed
> Interested in others
> Eager to share
> Never too busy to help
> Days spent with friends are special.

Entire Class

1. After showing the class an example of an acrostic poem, ask why they think an acrostic poem is an effective way to inform people about bullying.

Sample Answers

It's easy to write.

People will get the message twice, once through the words and then from the poem made from the words.

Writing it is fun because it's a challenge.

2. Have the class generate sample title words to use for acrostic poems. Ask students to choose the best ten word or words from this list to write their poems with groups or partners.

Small Groups

1. Students write acrostic poems using the words from the class list.

2. After writing the poems, students transfer them to poster boards and illustrate them with drawings. Students read and display posters.

Individuals

1. Students write and illustrate their own one or two word acrostic poems related to bullying problems or solutions.

Examples

think
care
look strong
hang on

2. Display students' poems throughout the school for other classes to read.

ACTIVITY 36

Make Up a Wish List
for a Better World

Description: With your group, think of ways that the world would be a better place without bullying. Using your best idea, write a creative message to exchange with another class about what it would be like to live in a bully-free world or school. Write a paragraph stating your own unique plan for stopping bullying.

Teaches: Character education (discussing with parents music that reflects a bully-free world); thinking of reasons to stop bullying; sharing ideas with another class about the benefits of not bullying; and using the newspaper as a vehicle to voice ideas about bullying.

Helpful Hints:

Arrange with another teacher of any grade level you choose to exchange short messages with the class about what it would be like to live in a bully-free world (or school).

After groups complete their messages, have the two classes meet and exchange ideas.

Entire Class

1. Ask the class to talk to their parents about music that would reflect a world without bullying. Have volunteers bring in samples of their parents' music and their own music that reflect a peaceful world.

2. Play and discuss some of the selections, and ask how the songwriter depicts a peaceful world or a world without bullying.

3. Ask the class to brainstorm how the world would improve if no one (children or adults) bullied others.

Sample Answer

If no one bullied others, the world would improve because people would treat one another with respect and dignity. They would appreciate differences in people and never treat one another disrespectfully because they looked, believed, or spoke differently. The world would be a better place if people did not hurt others' feelings or hurt them physically by bullying them. If enough people did their part to stop bullying, we could see this dream happen; it's up to us.

Small Groups

1. Have students meet in groups to write creative messages about what it would be like to live in a bully-free school or world. At the end of their messages, groups will write one thing they can do to make bullying less of a problem in the world or in their school.

Sample Messages

Life would be a dream in a bully-free world. To make that dream real, speak out when you see a bully bothering someone.

A bully-free school would be a school where everyone could relax and not worry that a bully will tease, hit, or harass children. We can each do our part by treating everyone with kindness and respect.

2. Students exchange messages with groups from another class. Have the groups write responses about the messages to the groups that wrote them.

3. Send selected messages to a local or city newspaper explaining your project and ask if the paper would like to publicize the project by printing sample messages.

Individuals

Ask individuals to write a paragraph listing their own unique plan for stopping bullying in the world or the school. Students share ideas.

ACTIVITY 37

Help a Younger Child with a Bullying Problem

Description: Write a dialogue that shows advice you'd give a younger child about what to do if a bully strikes. Make it short, interesting, and meaningful. Write an essay about a bullying episode, or write words you would say to encourage a younger child living with bullying.

Teaches: Character Development (helping a younger child with a bullying problem and learning to listen when helping others).

Helpful Hints: Explain that a dialogue is a conversation between two people. Tell students to give both people a chance to say what they're thinking. Stress having the people talk to each other rather than having the older student tell the younger child what to do.

Entire Class

1. Have the class cite examples they've seen of younger children being bullied in school or in the neighborhood. Ask if they've ever seen an older child attempt to help stop the bullying. What did the older child do to help? How did that child's actions help the younger child?

2. Ask the class what they would say to help a younger child experiencing bullying.

Sample Answers

Things to Say to a Younger Child

"I see someone is bothering you. Can I help?"

"Let's talk about how to handle this."

"You don't have to take that from those kids. Let's see what we can do about it."

"I can give you some ideas to help you deal with what's going on."

"It looks like things are getting worse. We need to talk to an adult about this."

Small Groups

1. Have students meet in groups to write dialogues between an older and younger child

Sample Situation

The older child witnesses the student facing a problem with a bully and tries to help the younger child during and after the episode. After the episode, the younger and older child talk about what the younger child can do to prevent further bullying.

2. Students act out their dialogues for the class with one or more students portraying the bully, and others portraying the younger child and the older child. Tell them to feel free to add other characters.

3. After students act out their dialogues, ask the class to comment on the ideas shown to help the younger child deal with bullying. Which ones do they think would work best and why?

Individuals

1. (*Option 1*) Ask students to write an essay about a bullying episode that they or another person experienced in the past. If anyone helped them, what did the person do to help stop the bully? Use fictitious names.

Sample Essay

When I was in fifth grade, a group of kids started making fun of me because I didn't move fast enough in the relay race. We had teams for Spirit Day, and some kids on my team said I kept them from winning. For the next few days, they called me *pokey turtle* and *loser*. I tried ignoring them, but things got worse. A friend suggested I talk to Evan, the boy we thought was the leader of the group. I tried talking to him, but he wouldn't listen.

I felt I had no choice but to talk to my counselor, Ms. Patel. She decided to call Evan in. She said that since he and his friends continued to cause a problem after I talked to him, it was time for her to get involved. We talked about what happened and how it had to stop. After a few sessions with the counselor, who talked to both our parents, the boy and his friends stopped calling me names.

I think Evan and I both learned something. I learned that if bullying keeps up and I can't handle it myself, there's no shame in asking for support. Hopefully, Evan learned that our school won't put up with bullying and that the staff do everything they can to stop it.

2. (*Option 2*) Ask students to write words that they would say to a younger child facing a bully. They should tell how the child is being bullied and what advice they would give the child.

Sample Answer

My name is Shayna, and my sister Emily is in your class. I met you when you visited my sister at our house. Emily told me some girls are texting nasty things about you and are spreading rumors on the Internet. I don't think you can handle this yourself; I don't think anybody could. I'll go with you to the principal if you want. We're going to solve this problem, and it will stop. It may take some time, but it's going to end. Please call me, Sarah, and let me know what you think of my idea.

3. Volunteers share essays with the class.

ACTIVITY 38

Write an Imaginary Bully a Letter

Description: Write an imaginary bully a letter. State the problem and tell how you want the bully to stop bothering you.

Teaches: Using letter writing to seek solutions to a bullying problem and considering how tone in speech or writing affects communications with others.

Helpful Hints:

Discuss: What would be the advantages and disadvantages of writing a bully a letter?

Sample Answers

Advantages	Disadvantages
You can tell the bully exactly how you feel.	The bully might laugh, show people your letter, or get angry.
The bully may spend time thinking about his or her actions.	The bully may not read your letter.
It's less emotional than trying to talk to the bully directly.	The bully may not want to hear from you at all.
The bully may reconsider what he or she is doing.	The bully may not want to change.

When would writing a letter or talking to the bully not be a helpful thing to do?

Sample Answer

It would not be a good idea if the bully teases you constantly, gets physical, or treats you cruelly. It would be best to write a letter to the bully only with the counselor's knowledge and supervision. Then you and the bully could discuss the letter with the counselor present.

On the other hand, writing an imaginary letter might help because it helps you understand how you feel about the bullying and may motivate you to start a plan of action against the way the bully's treating you.

Entire Class

1. Ask students if they have ever told a bully what they were thinking about the way the bully treated them. Did it help or hurt the situation?

2. Ask students if there is any circumstance in which they would not write or tell the bully how the bullying is affecting them. If they wouldn't, how would they feel about writing a letter and not sending it? Do they think it would help them think about new things to try in a bullying situation? Could writing a letter and not sending it help in any way?

3. If students could tell the bully what they were thinking and feeling in a letter, what kinds of things would they write?

Small Groups

1. Ask groups or partners to compose a letter to an imaginary bully, telling how they feel about the bully's actions. They will tell the bully why they won't accept bullying in the future.

Sample Letter

To Alex:

    I want you to know that I don't like it when you tell the other kids I'm dumb and call me names. You may not think I'm as smart or popular as you, but there are a lot of things I do well, like fix cars and play basketball.

    I know you wouldn't like it if other kids did that to you. I want you to stop saying bad things about me and calling me names. We may never be friends, but I'd like you to treat me as you'd want people to treat you.

Sincerely,

Miguel

2. Have students read their letters to the class and ask the class to say what they liked about each letter.

Individuals

1. Discuss how tone shows the way a person says something or intends it to sound to the reader. Practice saying the same words in different tones of voice to give your words different effects. How can tone affect the meaning of your writing?

2. Ask students to write a second letter to an imaginary bully, asking the bully to stop and think before teasing or hurting another person. They will write their letters in a positive, yet firm tone.

ACTIVITY 39

Sell a Children's Book about Bullying

Description: Read a fiction or nonfiction book about bullying. Write and deliver a book report with the aim of selling your book to the class and inspiring students to read it.

Teaches: Character education (intergenerational communication); using techniques from advertising to promote books; discussing books related to bullying; and building a reading list of books about bullying.

Helpful Hints:

Ask the class to look at TV commercials or to listen to radio commercials with a parent or grandparent. Ask them to discuss with their family members what the actors in the commercials say and do to get people to buy products. Students report back to the class on their findings.

Ask the class what they might do to encourage others to read a helpful book about bullying. How would they sell the book to their classmates using some advertising techniques?

Entire Class

1. Ask students to find a fiction or nonfiction book about bullying that appeals to them. In about four weeks, they will give short (five-to-ten minute) individual reports to the class with the aim of making the report so interesting that everyone will want to read book.

2. Ask the class to submit titles to you before reading the book so that you can check the content and grade level to see if the book would appeal to your students.

Small Groups

Have groups develop a list of suggestions based on their conversations with parents about commercials, along with their own ideas, for making their reports informative and dynamic.

Sample List

Read a short passage from the most interesting part of the book to excite the class about reading the book.

Discuss the theme of the book and show how it can help children with bullying problems.Have class members ask the presenters tough questions about the book.

Pretend you're the author pitching the book at a book signing.

Groups discuss their ideas and refine the suggestions, choosing the best ones.

Individual students make note of the group's best ideas and use them in their presentations to the class.

Individuals

1. Students write and deliver their reports to the class, paying particular attention to the main message of the book, gaining class interest by reading a short but interesting segment from the book, and promoting the book by using an enthusiastic tone and body language.

2. The class asks the presenters questions and discusses individual reports.

ACTIVITY 40

Peer Counsel a Bully

Description: Imagine that your teacher or counselor asks you to talk to a bully about how he or she has hurt another child. Think of five things you'd say to the bully to help the person think differently about bullying. With your group, write skits showing what you'd say to a bully. Pretend a bully is teasing your friend. Write a script of what to say.

Teaches: Things to say to someone bullying another child and when to talk or not talk to a bully.

Helpful Hints:

Discuss why you think bullies bother other children. What do they gain by it?

Discuss: Do you think that a bully would listen to another child rather than an adult when it comes to convincing the bully to stop doing things to hurt others? Why or why not?

Ask the class: If you could talk to a bully, do you feel that it should be one on one, with other children around, or with an adult present? Under what circumstances would you not discuss a bully's actions with the bully?

Entire Class

1. Discuss with the class: If you could talk to a bully about how his or her actions hurt another child, what kinds of things would you say? Ask the

class to tell which of the ideas they'd use and why. Write all suggestions on the board and put a star next to the best ones.

Sample Answers

"I don't like how you're acting."
"Stop bothering my friend."
"Stop saying that."
"Think about how you would feel."
"You need to stop saying those things."

2. Ask the class what kind of body language they'd use when talking to the bully.

Sample Answers

Look strong and powerful.
Make eye contact with the bully but don't stare.
Stand straight and still and don't move around.
Keep your voice steady, talking at a normal pace.

3. Have students demonstrate helpful and unhelpful body language.

Small Groups

1. Ask groups to create mini-plays (five to ten minutes each) about talking to a bully about how he or she has hurt another child. One child plays the bully and another plays the child talking to the bully. Groups can also cast students in the role of a teacher, counselor, or school administrator.

2. Groups perform their plays for the class. The class tells why they think talking to the bully in the way demonstrated would or wouldn't work.

Individuals

Suppose a bully is teasing your friend. Write a script of what you would say to the bully to convince him or her to stop. Volunteers read scripts to the class.

ACTIVITY 41

Pretend You're the Mayor

Description: As an elected official, present a community service award to a student who has helped stop a person from being bullied. Write a response to "the mayor's" speech.

Teaches: Character education (community involvement); the importance of taking a stand on bullying; and writing speeches to highlight involvement in bully prevention.

Helpful Hints:

Ask the class why they think the mayor would give an award to a child who has stopped another child from being bullied.

Sample Answers

To show how important an issue bullying is
To show other children that they can help stop bullying
To help others see the child as someone performing an important service

Discuss who else could present an award for stopping a bullying problem.

Sample Answers

teacher
counselor

157

principal
newspaper editor

Which of these people, including the mayor, do you think could most help bring attention to the problem and why?

Entire Class

1. **Discuss**: If you were the mayor, what positive things would you say about a person who stopped a bullying problem?

Sample Answers

"I consider this young person a hero."
"He took a stand and showed courage."
"She spoke out while others watched and said nothing."
"He set a positive example for our school."
"She took a giant step toward creating a bully-free school."

2. Ask the class what kinds of things they would say to stress the importance of everyone showing concern when someone is bullied.

3. Have the class debate whether they would consider a person who stopped a bullying problem a hero.

Small Groups

1. Ask groups to write a short but interesting speech for the mayor who will give an award to a person who helped stop bullying in a small or large way.

2. Have the groups choose a person in each group whom they think will most effectively deliver the mayor's speech. One student plays the part of the mayor, and another plays the recipient of the award.

3. Groups deliver speeches, and recipients of the award respond briefly, telling what it meant to them to help a bullying victim.

Individuals

1. Students write a response to one of "the mayor's" speeches, telling why bullying is everyone's problem and why everyone must do something to stop it. Post the best responses.

Sample Response

Bullying affects everyone and is everyone's business. Whenever we see someone teasing, name calling, hitting, or ignoring someone, we need to do something to stop it. If we stand by and don't help a bullying victim, the bullying may spread or continue. It may even affect us, so we must all be heroes, even in a small way, and help stop the bullying.

Write a Child's Picture Book about Bully Prevention

Description: Use words and pictures to teach children younger than you how to deal with bullies. Write a picture book with your group. Read the book to someone you think could learn from your message.

Teaches: Character development (empathy, social awareness, and helping younger children with bullying problems by writing and reading stories).

Helpful Hints:

Discuss with the class what types of bullying they have seen younger children experience.

If they were to write a picture book about bullying for a younger child, what types of things would they consider for the plot of the story?

Suggested Answers

Describe the problem.
Tell what the child has done to help solve the problem.
Talk about what more the child can do to solve the problem.
Show the child finding a solution.

Entire Class

1. Ask how reading stories to children might help them cope with bullying problems.

2. Go over plot structure. Every story must have a beginning, middle, and end. Advise students to give this book a positive ending that shows the child winning and the bully losing.

3. Ask the class how they would get a message across or give advice in a story without telling someone what to do or sounding like they're lecturing.

4. Have students list bullying situations they would like to write about in a picture book for younger children. Write them on the board and ask them to choose the best ideas. See that there are more ideas than there are groups.

Small Groups

1. Ask groups to decide on a plot and theme for a story and to write a short picture book about bullying for younger children. Group members who enjoy art can illustrate the books with their own drawings or pictures cut from magazines.

2. After writing a rough draft and having it approved, groups will revise their stories.

3. Groups will take turns reading their books to the entire class and will display them in the classroom.

4. Selected groups may also visit a class of younger students and read their picture books to the class.

5. Send completed books to the counselor, who will use them with younger students facing bullying.

Individuals

After hearing all the stories, students will write a brief evaluation of one story, stating why they think it would help younger students experiencing bullying. Students summarize their evaluations for the class.

Plaster a Wall with a Bully-busting Display

Description: Create oversized displays with bully-busting tips and post them in hallways to create a backdrop for a bully-free school.

Teaches: Character development (helping to create a bully-free school climate); school safety awareness; brainstorming to find solutions to bullying; and combining writing and art to create an anti-bully message.

Helpful Hints:

Ask the class how posting prominent bully prevention displays in the hallways could help create a safer school.

Have the class discuss other hallway displays that have caught their attention. What did they like best about the displays, and how could they use some of these ideas to create their own displays?

Entire Class

1. Have the class discuss formats for their displays (messages and illustrations) that would make students notice them and think more about problems caused by bullying.

2. Have students brainstorm bully-busting tips, and write them on the board. Students vote for the best ten or twelve tips. Place a star next to these tips.

Small Groups

1. Ask groups to choose two tips to use in their displays. They can use large poster board or long sheets of paper. They will reword the ideas the class composed in a lively, interesting way that will make students want to read and apply the advice.

2. Groups use colorful illustrations to complement their ideas. All groups will work together to plan and coordinate their bully-busting recommendations into a schoolwide display.

3. Invite other classes to view the class's display and to send short feedback messages about it to a designated class member.

Individuals

1. Students make a list of other things their class and other classes can do to work together to create a bully-free school. They will then expand their best idea into a paragraph.

Sample Answers

Ask the counselor to join with a group of students to give an assembly about bullying.

Ask the principal to invite the author of a book about bullying to speak at your school.

With the help of the counselor, start a support group to fight bullying.

Ask your teacher to use bullying as a topic for reading, writing, or speaking assignments.

Write your best bully-prevention tips on slips of paper, and ask teachers to discuss them in class.

2. Students pitch their ideas to the class and decide collectively on another project to bring bully-prevention to the school's attention.

Imagine You Are a Teacher Who Wants to Stop a Bullying Problem

Description: A bully is bothering someone in your class. What could the teacher say to stop the problem? Write a script.

Teaches: Learning about the different roles adults play in bully prevention; understanding the part teachers play in dealing with bullying; and expressing opinions on how teachers can further help stop bullying in the school.

Helpful Hints: Ask how different adults (parents, teachers, counselors, principals, and bus drivers) can help with bullying problems.

Sample Answers

Parents

Parents can ask their children what's going on in school if they seem overly quiet, sad, or irritable.

If their children don't want to go to school, parents should ask why they want to stay home.

They can tell their children that they can talk to them about anything that's bothering them and listen, giving them as much time as they need to discuss the problem.

They can discuss bullying and bully prevention tips with their children, starting at a young age, before they enter school.

(continued on next page)

Sample Answers
Teachers

Teachers can take action when they see children treating others unkindly.

They can hold class discussions about tolerance of students' differences and the importance of treating everyone with respect.

They can make bully prevention a part of their courses.

Sample Answers
Counselors

They can visit classrooms to discuss bully prevention.

They can help individual students with bullying problems.

They can talk to bullies about why bullying is wrong and try to get them to understand how it feels to be bullied.

They can discuss problems with parents of bullied children and those who bully.

Sample Answers
Principals

They can set the tone in school for harmony and respect among students.

They can provide a safe zone for bullied children, providing trained counselors or teachers for support.

They can set a zero tolerance policy for bullying in school, giving consequences every time one student bullies another.

They can hold open discussions about bully prevention and invite experts to speak.

They can form a partnership between home and school to stop bullying.

They can open their offices to students who want to discuss bullying.

Sample Answers
Bus Drivers

When the school year begins, bus drivers can clearly explain their positions about bullying on the bus. They can call to the principal's attention any bullying episodes.

They can contact students' parents about bullying problems.

They can be aware of and deal with bullying problems before they get worse.

Discuss how children can rely on each of the people mentioned above to help them if a bully bothers them. Stress that if one person is unwilling or unable to help, students should consult someone else.

Entire Class

1. Have the class discuss times they saw a teacher help stop a bullying problem. Why is the teacher an important part of the bully prevention team?

2. Discuss: Why do you think some teachers may not do anything when they see a bully bothering someone? Is it always important for a teacher to get involved?

Small Groups

1. Groups compose scripts showing a teacher talking to one student or a group of students who are bullying another student or students. As an alternative, groups could show the teacher talking to a class that has experienced the bullying of one or more students. Another scenario would involve the teacher advising someone being bullied.

2. When writing the script, remind students that the teacher will involve the student or students taking part in the bullying or going through the bullying, rather than simply telling them what to do.

3. Students perform their plays for the class, and the class comments on the plays, saying whether they think the ideas would work in real life.

Individuals

1. Have students write a short paper stating specific things they think the teacher can do to help stop bullying in school.

2. The actual teacher comments on how these ideas may help stop bullying in school and shares student comments with other teachers and administrators.

Think of Things to Say to a Bully

Description: Make a list of names you've heard bullies call people and different things bullies have said to hurt people's feelings. What kinds of things could you say to the person who has called you each of these names or has said hurtful things? Act out situations in which a bully calls a person names. Write a mini-story about a bully who name calls or says unkind things to another student.

Teaches: How to respond to a bully in a variety of circumstances; constructive ways to respond to a bully; deciding when not to respond to a bully; and evaluating the effectiveness of different responses to a bully.

Helpful Hints:

Discuss when it is best not to say something back to a bully.

Sample Answer

It's best not to say anything to a bully who seems threatening or who could hurt you physically. Also, if there's more than one person involved, it's best not to handle it yourself. Leave the scene, and find an adult to help you.

Remind the class that their examples of what bullies say needs to be "G" rated for classroom use.

Entire Class

1. Ask the class to discuss different names they have heard bullies call other children or different things bullies have said to belittle them.

2. What kinds of responses have they heard that they thought were helpful? Which ones didn't help?

Small Groups

1. Groups meet to act out short situations showing a bully name calling or saying hurtful things to another student. They show the student responding and the bully's reaction.

2. The class evaluates each presentation, telling why it would or would not work in real life.

Individuals

Write a mini-story about a bully who name calls or says unkind things to another student. How did the student help the problem or hurt it by the way he or she responded to the bully's put-downs? Assign a number to each student to ensure anonymity. Distribute stories to groups. Each group chooses one story to read to the class.

Sample Mini-story

Keith and Binh are sixth graders at the local middle school. Keith started bullying Binh in grade school by teasing him about his short height. Now that they're older, Keith's bullying has turned crueler, and he picks on Binh more frequently, making fun of his glasses and braces. He also calls Binh's mother *ugly* and calls his sister *a fat cow*. He says Binh's father sounds stupid with his accent.

Keith has threatened to beat up Binh because he doesn't like his looks or anything about him. Binh has two good friends in class who have supported him by staying close by whenever Keith shows up. They also give him tips such as, "Look strong, talk like you're confident and not scared, and tell if you need to."

Whenever Keith starts pestering Binh, he tries one of his friends' suggestions. The bullying stops for a short time, but in a couple of days, Keith starts bothering Binh again. Because of Keith's threats and the fact that the bullying is getting worse, Binh decides to talk to his teacher and counselor about Keith's actions.

The teacher and counselor asked Keith to talk to them in the counselor's office. They didn't mention that Binh had said anything about Keith's actions. Instead, they said that someone told them about the bullying. The counselor set up separate appointments with Binh and Keith. For the next couple of weeks, they met with Keith and Binh to work toward a solution. Also, the teacher, counselor, and Binh's parents felt it best to change Binh's class because of how long the bullying went on and because of the threats. The bullying has finally stopped, and Binh feels much better.

Teach a Lesson on Bully Prevention to a Younger Class

Description: What are the most important things a younger child can say or do to keep a bully away? Plan a lesson in bully prevention and present it to a group of younger children. Develop a list of suggestions that younger children can use for bully prevention, and display them on a poster.

Teaches: Character development (concern for others); using family members as a resource for bully prevention; and finding ways to help younger children prevent bullying.

Helpful Hints:

Ask the class to remember when they were younger and experienced bullying or saw someone go through it. How did they react to it? What helped and what didn't help?

Have students talk to younger relatives to find out what types of bullying they've experienced and how they handled it. Which things that they did worked best? Students will report their findings to the class.

Entire Class

1. Have students list bullying scenarios that younger children might experience. Next to each situation, they will list ways to prevent or stop the bullying. Make a chart on the board.

2. Discuss solutions listed on the board, asking students to cross out solutions they think won't work and to put stars next to the most favorable ones.

3. Have each group choose different situations and solutions and base their lesson plan for a younger class on one of these situations.

4. Discuss what makes a lesson interesting. Ask how students can make their presentations appealing to a younger class.

Sample Answers

Introduce the topic with dramatic examples of bullying you've heard about from younger students.

Don't talk too much. Let the students discuss the subject and ask you questions.

Give all students a chance to talk, and don't let a few students take over the discussion.

Set two or three rules for behavior at the beginning of the class, such as "Listen when someone else is talking" and "Respect one another's opinions even if you don't agree with them."

Small Groups

1. Groups plan mini-lessons (five to ten minutes) about bully prevention and/or solutions for younger students. They should plan for audience participation and create lively and positive presentations geared to the class's age level.

2. Arrange with a teacher of younger students to present one or more lessons to the class. As an alternative, groups could spread their lessons among two or more classes so that all groups would have a chance to present their lessons.

Individuals

1. Ask students to compose a list of practical suggestions that younger children could use for bully prevention and for stopping a bully's actions.

2. Discuss suggestions with the class and write them on the board. Ask the class to vote on the twenty best suggestions. Volunteers who excel in art will create and illustrate one or more posters based on the suggestions. Students will donate the posters to classes of younger students when they teach their lessons.

ACTIVITY 47

Exchange Ideas to Stop Bullying Outside of School

Description: On 3 × 5 cards, your group names different ways they've seen a bully bother someone outside of school. Exchange the cards with another group. Take turns saying what you would do to stop the bully in each of the situations. Write about bullying outside of school and what you think would help the problem.

Teaches: Thinking quickly about how to react to a bully and thinking about solutions for bullying outside of school.

Helpful Hints:

Ask the class why brainstorming with groups often helps people think of better ideas than if they tried to come up with them on their own.

Discuss why the first idea that comes to mind about solving a problem is often the best one.

Entire Class

1. Ask students if they think that bullying outside of school is easier or harder to fight than in-school bullying. Have them give reasons for their positions.

2. Ask the class to name different places they've seen a bully bother people outside of school. List the situations on the board. Why can out-of-school bullying cause more problems than school bullying?

Sample Answer

> Bullies bother other children in public parks, playgrounds, and basketball courts. They also bother them in movie theaters, restaurants, and malls. Basically, they tease, name call, and ignore other children in these locations. These situations can cause more problems than school bullying because sometimes there is no one around to help if the bullying gets out of hand.

2. Groups will use these and other situations as the bases for their idea exchange with another group.

Small Groups

1. Groups write situations on 3 × 5 cards, listing as many situations as there are students in the group.

2. Groups exchange cards with another group, which will brainstorm solutions to each bullying situation. Groups discuss and refine their responses to the bullying situations before writing them on the cards. After groups write solutions, they will return the cards to the original groups.

3. Groups that originally wrote the situations share what they wrote, along with the other group's answers, with the class. The class discusses responses to each situation, commenting on the possible effectiveness of each solution. Suggest this wording: "I think this would (or would not) work because . . . "

Individuals

What is the worst out-of-school bullying situation you've seen, heard, or read about? Write about what you think might have helped stop this problem sooner. Discuss ideas with the class.

Pull the Mask from Invisible Bullies

Description: These bullies are out there, but you can't always see what they're doing to hurt others. Groups act out situations with invisible bullies, and the class responds with ideas for fighting this type of bullying.

Teaches: Understanding how an "invisible bully" can hurt others and learning when and how to react to an invisible bully.

Helpful Hints:

Talk about how an "invisible bully" can hurt people.

Discuss when it's best to say something or not to react if an invisible bully treats you unkindly.

Entire Class

1. Discuss what makes a bully invisible. What kinds of things can bullies say or do behind the scenes that other people might not notice.

Examples

Excluding others from their group
Ignoring people
Talking or laughing behind other children's backs
Writing unkind things about others in notes or on the Internet

2. Have students discuss specific cases of invisible bullying they've observed that others might not have noticed.

Examples

Jen texts her friends, telling them to ignore Maria because she doesn't fit in with the group

Sean convinces his friends to exclude Tyrone from a football game because he doesn't score enough points

Theresa passes a note to Liz in math class, telling her not to invite Anna to her party because she's ugly and unpopular.

Small Groups

1. Ask groups to write short scenes featuring an invisible bully or bullies doing one of the things the class mentioned in its discussion. They may also use an original idea.

2. Groups will depict the invisible bully or bullies bothering someone but will not give the victim's reaction.

Individuals

1. Students will watch the groups' enactment of the scenes and then comment on how they would respond to the bully or bullies if they were the bully's targets.

2. The class will discuss various ways to approach each situation and will state whether they would respond or not respond to the bully's actions.

Compile a Vocabulary List of Bullying Terms

Description: Use a dictionary to look up words related to bullying and ideas to stop bullying. Make up a word search, crossword puzzle, or jumbled word game using the words and definitions. Using five bullying terms, write an essay about bullying.

Teaches: Knowledge of bully-related terms; using a variety of sources to research bullying terms; learning about bullying terms by working with word puzzles; and reinforcing bullying terminology by using these words in an essay.

Helpful Hints:

Discuss the importance of understanding bullying terms.

Ask the class to list resources they can use to find definitions for bullying terms (dictionary, thesaurus, nonfiction books, and the Internet). Younger children can use a children's dictionary and thesaurus.

Entire Class

1. Have the class list terms they've heard or read about that relate to bullying

Examples

bully
bystander

> teasing
> tattling
> aggression
> threats
> rumors
> zero tolerance
> school safety
> responsible adult
> cyber bullying

2. For more ideas, students can look in the index of age-appropriate nonfiction books about bullying.

2. Ask students to phrase definitions of terms in a vocabulary that matches their grade level. Write words and definitions on the board.

3 Discuss ways to compose different types of puzzle activities such as word searches, crossword puzzles, and jumbled word games (students unscramble two or three words and then solve a puzzle to make one word out of the circled letters of the jumbled words). Ask students for more suggestions for using the vocabulary definitions in word games.

Small Groups

1. Students use the terms and definitions on the board and some of their own to create the word games listed above. Each group composes one word game and provides an answer key for its game.

2. Groups write their names on the puzzle but do not write the answers on the puzzles. They exchange puzzles with another group, who will work out the puzzles and return the completed puzzle to the group that created it. The puzzle inventors will check the answers and fill in incorrect answers in red before returning the puzzle to those who worked on it.

Individuals

1. Students will write a short essay about bullying using at least five of the bullying terms listed on the board, and they will underline the terms.

Sample Essay

A *bully* shows *aggression* in many different ways. He or she uses *teasing,* ignoring, or hitting to hold power over another person. We can fight bullying by learning bully-prevention tips and practicing them. We can show bullies that we won't accept mistreatment. If we can't handle the bully's actions, it's important to tell a *responsible adult.* Parents, teachers, students, and principals need to make *school safety* an important goal if they want to stop bullying.

2. Display essays in the hallway so that other students will learn bullying terms.

Stop Cyber Bullying

Description: Use a search engine to look up types of cyber bullying, and give examples you've heard or read about in the news media. Think of things people can do to stop cyber bullying, and report back to the class. Write a fiction story about cyber bullying.

Teaches: How cyber bullying takes place; the prevalence of cyber bullying and how it affects people; ways of dealing with cyber bullying; and educating parents about cyber bullying.

Helpful Hints:

Discuss where cyber bullying takes place.

Examples

e-mails
instant messages
text messages
chat rooms
websites
blogs

Ask the class to discuss why cyber bullying is an extremely dangerous type of bullying.

Entire Class

1. Discuss whether students have heard or read about any episodes of cyber bullying and have them explain what happened.

2. Ask the class what they, their parents, and the school can do to help prevent cyber bullying.

Sample Answers

Students can help prevent cyber bullying by not responding to e-mails, text messages, and blogs that feature unkind or malicious remarks or rumors. They can bring cyber bullying to the counselor's or principal's attention.

Parents can supervise their children's Internet activity by keeping in close touch with their children and by seeing if they give or receive any suspicious messages from Internet sources. If they learn their child is the person who sends or receives cyber bullying, they should act quickly to solve the problem.

The *School* can help by discussing cyber bullying in classrooms and assembly programs. A school administrator can invite a member of the police department to talk about cyber bullying, the problems it creates, and the penalties connected with it.

2. Ask the students what they would do if someone used cyber bullying on them or a friend.

Small Groups

1. Ask groups to explain to the class why they believe cyber bullying hurts others and to brainstorm three things they can do to help stop cyber bullying.

2. Groups set up an information table on parents' visitation night to inform parents about cyber bullying.

Individuals

1. Students write a short fiction story in the third person about a cyber-bullying incident, telling what happened, how it hurt the person being bullied, and what happened to solve the problem.

Sample Story

Isabel was in the popular group in her class until Celia, the group leader, became jealous of her when she won the award for the highest class average. Celia started telling the other girls that Isabel became conceited since winning the award in a school assembly. Isabel felt hurt and betrayed by Celia and could not understand why she would spread that story about her. But Celia would not listen and said more unkind things about her.

Celia also told her friends to ignore Isabel and to exclude her from get-togethers at their houses. The other girls agreed because they were afraid that they would not be a part of the group if they went against Celia. Isabel felt sad that the girls she thought were her friends dropped her from their group because of what Celia had said. But she moved forward and easily made new friends.

One day Tamika, one of her new friends, told Isabel that she looked on a popular website and saw a picture of her posted with some false stories written under her name. Isabel became upset and told her mother she didn't feel well so that she wouldn't have to go to school. Her mother couldn't get her to talk about what bothered her until Mr. Robinson, Isabel's homeroom teacher, called her mother and told her he'd heard from Tamika that some girls were spreading rumors about her on the website.

Isabel's mother looked at the website; then she told her daughter she knew about it and that they needed to talk. Isabel's mother contacted the principal and the school police officer, who spoke to Celia's parents about how Celia was using the Internet to bully Isabel.

Once everything was out in the open, Celia stopped spreading lies about Isabel. The school police officer warned her that if the bullying started up again, she would contact the local police station and that Isabel's mother would press charges.

2. Ask a few students to read their stories to the class.

About the Author

Dr. Catherine DePino, a former teacher, disciplinarian, and department head of English and world languages in the Philadelphia School System, has written many books for teachers, two spiritual books for teenagers, and a chapter book, *Blue Cheese Breath and Stinky Feet: How to Deal with Bullies.* She wrote *101 Activities to Help Your Preschooler Excel in Reading, Writing, and Speaking* to help teachers and parents jumpstart their children's verbal skills. Her latest chapter book, *In Your Face, Pizza Face: A Girl's Bully-Busting Book*, addresses the topic of relational aggression. Her forthcoming book, *Elliot K. Carnucci is a Big, Fat Loser,* tells the story of a ninth grader who faces relentless bullying by his peers. The author also serves on the board of directors of The Philadelphia Writers Conference.